T0198017

Building Websites for a Multinational Audience

Linda Main

The Scarecrow Press, Inc.
Lanham, Maryland, and Oxford
2002

SCARECROW PRESS, INC.

Published in the United States of America
by Scarecrow Press, Inc.
A Member of the Rowman & Littlefield Publishing Group
4720 Boston Way, Lanham, Maryland 20706
www.scarecrowpress.com

PO Box 317
Oxford
OX2 9RU, UK

British Cataloging in Publication Information Available

Library of Congress Cataloging-in-Publication Data

Main, Linda.
  Building websites for a multinational audience / Linda Main.
    p. cm.
Includes bibliographical references and index.
  ISBN 0-8108-4503-2 (pbk. : alk. paper)
  1. Web sites—Design. 2. Multiculturalism. I. Title.
  TK5105.888.M3437 2002
  005.7'2—dc21

                                                        2002008066

Contents

Preface

Connecting Cyberspace: How to Build Websites for a Multinational Audience

Our increasingly electronically networked world reflects the diversity of information environments into which products and information are distributed and the special populations they serve. The office-, library-, and store-without-walls have become the working and recreational environments of the twenty-first century. A thoughtful website designer always considers what a user values and what the user's goal is when accessing a site. However, culture, language, and geography greatly influence a user's concepts and behaviors. Even within the United States, communities increasingly consist not only of long-term U.S. residents fluent in English, but of recent immigrants from places as different as Mexico, numerous Asian countries, and India. In the 2000 census, the number of people in the United States who do not speak English at home had risen to 45 million.

A successful website presents information to a user in a format to which he or she is accustomed. It is, however, an incredible challenge to build a website that can address the information needs of racially, ethnically, and linguistically diverse populations. The website designer must always remember that although he or she is thinking in terms of the global reach of the website, the user is coming to the website from a local perspective. This book tries to bring together the practical issues that should be considered by anyone building a website aimed at a multinational audience. It is a practical hands-on look at such issues as understanding writing systems, character sets, encoding, and Unicode; using XHTML and CSS stylesheets to build globalized web pages; the sensible use of graphics; and the possible uses of JavaScript, XML, and XSLT. Important subjective and objective cultural issues are also examined. The book is aimed at those who know how to build a basic website but wish to focus on globalizing their web pages and those who may outsource the building of their websites but wish to understand at least some of the issues and techniques involved in building a globalized website. The references and bibliographies bring together supporting material pulled from a wide variety of resources. Code examples from the chapters can be found at senna.sjsu.edu/lmain/global.

1

A Networked World

Huis Toe Blad (n) Home Page(Afrikaans)

Thuisplaat (n) Home Page (Danish)

Die Leitseite (n) Home Page (German)

ホームページ (n) Home Page (Japanese)

Pagina Principal (n) Home Page (Spanish)

Hemsida (n) Home Page (Swedish)

Addef Dudalen (n) Home Page (Welsh)

A HISTORICAL PRIME MOVER

A historical prime mover is an event or a technology that is not only important in itself, but also influences the development of yet more new technology and sends society in new directions. Writing and the printing press fall into this category. Not only were both new forms of technology, but they also impacted the world of ideas directly by creating a space in which new forms of expression could flourish. Like the development of both writing and the printing press, the Internet—and particularly the web—is a technology that impacts other technologies. It has brought about a significant shift in both the manner and speed with which information is distributed. Goods have always moved. People have always moved. Ideas have

1

always moved. Cultures have always changed. However, it took television 13 years, and the telephone 75 years, to acquire 50 million users; it took the Internet 5 years.

Since online users perceive that they do not have to identify themselves ethnically, religiously, or politically, they feel free to influence, discuss, and resolve issues and policies that impact their varied communities. The interconnectivity offered by the Internet has enabled minority groups to share their struggles with the rest of the world, most notably in Mexico, the former USSR, and the Balkans. It is interesting that most countries that have allowed Internet access have tolerated freer expression online than is permitted in the local news media. Stories that newspapers have declined to publish due to political pressure have circulated widely on the Internet. It has become a headquarters for every type of political action, from plans for corporate boycotts to tactical deliberations. It is used in disputes all over the world, from Peru to Ecuador to the Tibetan Information Network out of London distributing information to Tibetan exiles. It is used to support separatists in Chechnya, Nigeria, and East Timor. Citizens of Arab countries have debated and conversed with Israelis in chat rooms and online forums during times when face-to-face contact is difficult or impossible. It has also helped relief efforts in such places as Kobe, Japan. In Denmark, all public authorities have an e-mail box to which all citizens and companies can send letters. The Internet appears to have the potential of fulfilling the philosopher Isaiah Berlin's belief that the members of a society should strive not to agree with each other, but to understand each other. Of course, while we can argue that the Internet opens up the world as never before, it can also be used to promote propaganda and hate and to legitimize oppressive regimes that use it to market themselves to the world.

The World Bank stresses that, increasingly, the Internet is also becoming a prerequisite for economic development. The competitiveness of developing countries depends on their ability to exchange information globally. Companies that can quickly access information about conditions in export markets can respond rapidly to changing prices. An excellent example is the Cocoa Board in Ghana and the Ivory Coast, which has used the Internet to tie its cocoa producers to customers in world markets. The Internet also allows companies, such as Importnow.com and Onenest.com, to open up geographically fragmented markets in places like Bangladesh, Papua New Guinea, and Gozo.

There has been a concern that the proliferation of the Internet, and in particular the web, will lead to cultural imperialism or Americanization, that there will be a homogenization or internationalization of culture favoring Western developed nations and their languages and values. However, the movement of localized communities and identities onto the networks has shown that the Internet actually benefits minority cultures and languages.[1] It is a cheap and easy way to communicate local, ethnic, religious, and national cultures to a worldwide audience. Political groups use the Internet to promote local interests and politics rooted in very historic place-governed issues, such as race, nation, territory, and language. As Geoff Walsham says, "The existing culture of a country will mediate globalisation processes in particular ways in specific contexts and, in turn, this will contribute to the complexity of globalisation as a totality."[2]

IMPLICATIONS FOR THE WEBSITE DESIGNER

As early as 1997, Lehder, Millen, and Schriefer stressed the importance of making a website accessible to a multicultural, multinational audience. They listed the following reasons:

- From a business perspective, small companies can easily create a global presence by internationalizing their websites. Conversely, large companies may appear less competitive than they really are by ignoring internationalization issues.
- The market for a company is typically no longer limited to a single country.
- Companies are finding partners outside of their own countries.
- Companies have remote locations in various countries.[3]

The need to make a website appealing both in terms of appearance and content to a multicultural, multinational audience is even more pressing today. Our increasingly networked world reflects the diversity of information environments into which products and information are distributed, the special populations they serve, and the multidisciplinary and multicultural nature of the knowledge base on which they need to draw. Even within the United States, there is the challenge of making a website appeal to a diverse group of users ranging from long-term English-speaking U.S. residents to recent immigrants from various countries of origin. The 1990 U.S. census stated that 32 million people in the United States did not speak English at home.[4] In the same year, Global Reach[5] estimated that over 13.5 million Americans accessed the Internet both in English and in their native languages (and many only in their native languages). According to the 2000 census, the number of people in the United States who did not speak English at home had risen to 45 million.[6]

Consider the following:

- In 2001 Global Reach estimated that just over 266 million people accessing the Internet came from countries where the primary language was not English. This figure is projected to rise to 560 million by 2003.[7]
- By 2005, about 70 percent of the Internet's users will speak a language other than English.[8]
- By 2005 Jupiter estimates that nearly three quarters of online users will reside outside of North America.[9]
- By 2004, according to Forrester Research, 50 percent of all online sales will be to customers outside the United States.[10]
- By 2005, ethnic groups within the United States will spend USD 3.1 billion on Internet access, which is almost as much as the entire amount spent on Internet access in the United States in 2000.[11]
- In a 1998 study, Forrester Research found that users stayed at a site twice as long and were three times as likely to make a purchase when content is presented in a cultural format to which they can relate. The same survey found that two-thirds of Internet surfers would click away from a site in another language.[12]
- A 2001 survey by Taylor Nelson Sofres Information Technology Division found that more companies in the United States (93%), Japan (60%), Singapore (61%), Denmark (75%), France (36%), and the United Kingdom (86%) were using the Internet to deal with customers than they were for internal purposes. The In-

ternet was heavily used for customer service, marketing, and knowledge management. The report concluded the following:

> Companies can no longer deal with the Internet solely within the context of their own country. A website is a modern corporate brochure. A website must be globalized in order to communicate effectively to a target market. If not, it is not a sound investment in terms of resources or time.[13]

- A 2000 survey of 1,000 websites by the Web of Culture found that while Asian companies typically post their websites in their native languages and English, and while European companies tend to post their websites in more than two languages, American companies tend to post their websites in English only.[14] A 2001 report from the Web of Culture found that only a small number of American companies have reached a level of multicultural awareness as reflected in their websites.[15]

It is not only for-profit companies that must consider multicultural issues in their website design.

- Many nonprofit organizations are global and have offices worldwide.
- Universities want to attract international students and disseminate information to a worldwide academic community.
- Librarians must design appropriate web-based communication channels that will address the information needs of increasingly racially, ethnically, and linguistically diverse communities. This is of crucial importance as often public libraries are the main source of Internet access and electronic literacy for many in their catchment communities. They must provide opportunities for second-generation and second-language learners to access sites in different languages.[16]
- The web also enables librarians to provide services to very small minority groups that fall below the criteria for formal collecting.
- As more and more websites use virtual agents for online shopping or as a replacement for human technical support and customer service representatives, it is crucial to pay attention to cultural differences in users' behavior when interacting with

these online agents. The same applies to the building of virtual reference desks by librarians.

A thoughtful website designer considers a user's goals and what the user values, then builds a website with easy navigation, a clear, simple, and consistent interface, and good feedback messages. However, since culture, language, and geography will greatly influence a user's concepts and behaviors, the website designer must also address these issues when designing and building a website. Culture, language, and national identity are barriers that must be overcome in order to ensure that all users can access and accept the web pages. Graphical depictions must be easily recognizable in all cultures. Facial expressions and gestures should not be confusing, rude, or interpreted differently by different cultures. Visual and audio feedback must be language-independent when communicating with the user.

INTERNATIONALIZATION AND LOCALIZATION

Making a website accessible to a multicultural or international audience entails much more than language translation. It involves, at least, internationalization—sometimes called globalization—and possibly localization. The word *international* means "across many nations"; it does not mean "foreign." Therefore, internationalization, or globalization,[17] is the process of eliminating culture-specific content from a website. An internationalized, or globalized, website makes content accessible to a multicultural and international audience by containing no information or jargon that requires a specific cultural context for understanding. The end product is as culturally and technically neutral as possible. The website can then more easily be localized for a specific culture or cultures as the need arises.

Localization is the process by which a website's content, look, and feel are developed to meet the needs of a particular audience, possibly in a particular locale.[18] A locale can be thought of as a geographical, political, or cultural group (or region) that shares some combination of geography, politics, or culture. Localization generally includes translation but also entails much more. Graphics and wording are tailored to a specific market, as are audio clips and online help. The site should show sensitivity and awareness of local customs, cultures, and holidays.

Software programmers have been dealing with these issues for some time.[19] Website designers and builders are now realizing that they too are facing a challenging set of design issues that include understanding character sets and encoding, using dynamic XHTML, and considering objective and subjective cultural concerns.

The following chapters assume the reader has:

1. A basic knowledge about designing and building websites;
2. Some degree of experience with the hypertext markup language (HTML) and cascading style sheets (CSS);
3. A current version of the Internet Explorer browser (IE 5.5 or IE 6);
4. A Windows platform.

NOTES

1. Patxi Juaristi and Andoni Barreña, "Minority Languages and Globalization" at korrika.ametza.com/english/gutxitu1.htm (accessed March 1, 2002).

2. Geoff Walsham, "IT, Globalisation and Cultural Diversity," in *Information Technology in Context,* eds. Chrisanthi Avgerou and Geoff Walsham (Burlington, Vt.: Ashgate, 2000), 291.

3. D. Z. Lehder, D. R. Millen, and A. E. Schriefer, *Global Use of the Internet —Eight Emerging Themes* (Holmdel, N.J.: AT&T User Experience Symposium, 1997).

4. U.S. Census Bureau, "Languages Spoken at Home by Persons 5 Years and Over, by State: 1990 Census" at www.census.gov/population/socdemo/language/table4.txt (accessed March 1, 2002).

5. Global Reach, "Global Internet Statistics: Sources & References" at www.glreach.com/globstats/refs.php3 (accessed March 1, 2002); Global Reach, "Evolution & Projections of Online Linguistic Populations" at www.glreach.com/globstats/evol.html (accessed March 1, 2002).

6. U.S. Census Bureau, "Supplementary Survey: Summary Tables," in *Census 2000* at factfinder.census.gov/servlet/BasicFactsServlet (accessed March 1, 2002). To find the table, select *Search.* Enter "Census 2000" in the *Select Year and Program* box. Enter "Language spoken at home" in the keyword box.

7. Global Reach, "Global Internet Statistics (by Language)" at www.glreach.com/globstats (accessed March 1, 2001).

8. James Heckman, "'International' in Internet Closes U.S. Lead." *Marketing News* 34 (4): 7–8 (February 14, 2000).

9. Dawn Gareiss, "Business on the World Wide Web," December 11, 2000, at www.informationweek.com/816/global.htm (accessed March 1, 2002).

10. James Eedes, "Multilingual Net" at www.futurecompany.co.za/2000/07/28/noteb.htm (accessed March 1, 2002).

11. Insight, "Web Portals, ISPs, IP Telephony and the Ethnic Consumer: Bridging the Digital Divide" at www.insight-corp.com (accessed March 1, 2002).

12. Evantheia Schibsted, "All the World in Stages," November 1999, at www.business2.com/articles/mag/print/0,1643,13228,FF.html (accessed March 1, 2002).

13. Taylor Nelson Sofres Information Technology Division, "International Survey Findings" at www.tnsofres.com/features_item.cfm?news_ID=25 (acessed March 1, 2002).

14. Web of Culture at www.webofculture.com (accessed March 1, 2002).

15. Web of Culture, "Global Web 2001 Report" at www.webofculture.com/report (accessed March 1, 2002).

16. Some of these issues were featured in Technology, Globalization and Multicultural Services in Libraries Conference, IFLA (Satellite Program), August 14–16, 2001, Buffalo, N.Y. See the website at libris.lib.buffalo.edu/iflabuffalo (accessed March 1, 2002).

17. Often referred to as *I18n,* which is shorthand for *internationalization.* The number *18* indicates the number of letters abbreviated.

18. Often referred to as *L10n,* which is shorthand for *localization.* The number *10* indicates the number of letters abbreviated.

19. Elisa del Galdo and Jakob Nielsen, eds., *International User Interfaces* (New York: Wiley, 1996); Bert Esselink, *A Practical Guide to Localization* (Philadelphia: Benjamins, 2000); Nadine Kano, *Developing International Software* (Redmond, Wash.: Microsoft Press, 1995); Tiziana Perinotti, *Courseware for the SW/Web Industry: Internationalization and Localization Guide* at www.tgpconsulting.com (accessed March 1, 2002).

REFERENCES

"Business on the World Wide Web." *Information Week,* December 11, 2000, 69, at www.informationweek.com/816/global.htm (accessed August 12, 2002).

Collins, Rosann Webb. "Software Localization for Internet Software: Issues and Methods." *IEEE Software* (March/April 2002): 74–79, at computer.org/software/so2002/s2toc.htm (accessed March 1, 2002).

Doughtery, Carter. "Going Global." *Washington Times,* April 24, 2000, at www.lisa.org/press/washington_times.html (accessed March 1, 2002).

Ishida, Richard. "Challenges in Designing International User Information" at www.xerox-emea.com/globaldesign/paper/paper1.htm (accessed March 1, 2002).

LISA (Localisation Industry Standards Association) FAQs at www.lisa.unige.ch/info_faqs.html (accessed March 1, 2002).

Preston, Holly Hubbard, and Udo Flohr. "Global from Day One." *Byte* 22 (3): 97–101 (March 1997).

Sawhney, M., and S. Mandel. "Go Global." *Business 2.0*, May 1, 2001, at www.business2.com/articles/mag/0,1640,13580,FF.html (accessed March 1, 2002).

Wilson, Bonita. "Special Issue on Digital Technology and Indigeneous Communities." *D-Lib Magazine* 8 (3) (March 2002), at www.dlib.org/dlib/march02/03contents.html (accessed March 1, 2002).

"Web Site Globalization." *Computerworld*, July 10, 2000, 56, at www.computerworld.com/managementtopics/ebusiness/story/0,10801,46812,00.html (accessed August 12, 2002).

2

Understanding Writing Systems, Character Sets, Encoding, and Fonts

WRITING SYSTEMS

E-mail and the web are based on written language. Writing is a form of communication using common symbols that are sent, received, and understood. As mentioned in chapter 1, the emergence of writing can be thought of as a historical prime mover in much the same way as fire or the development of the wheel: fire and the wheel gave man control of his physical environment; writing gave man control of his intellectual environment. The move to a written, as opposed to an oral, culture meant that man could store his comprehension of himself and his world outside of himself.

Writing systems consist of rules for creating a visual representation of language and can be broadly categorized into alphabet-based systems and ideograph-based systems. Alphabet-based systems are able to create a great number of words from a small set of letters. Ideograph-based systems, such as Japanese, Korean, and Chinese, require thousands of ideographs to capture the language because the ideographs represent concepts that must be combined to give meaning.

Japanese text is composed of four different scripts mixed together: Kanji ideographs derived from Chinese and used to write root words; two phonetic scripts called Hiragana and Katakana; and Nihongo. Hiragana is the most common script, with cursive rather than block-like letterforms. Katakana is mostly used to represent foreign words imported from languages other than Japanese. Nihongo is used for transliteration of Japanese words into the Latin alphabet. On average, 55 percent of Japanese text is written in Hiragana, 35 percent in Kanji, and 10 percent in Katakana.

Korean text also uses ideographs based on a set invented in China and called Hanja. However, Korean text can also be written using a phonetic writing system called Hangul. Hangul characters are formed by combining consonants and vowels that are often arranged in a square so that the group takes up the same space as a Hanja character. Hanja is used mostly to avoid confusion when Hangul would be ambiguous.

Chinese consists of characters taken from an ideographic script called Hanzi. This set of ideographs is often referred to as Han because it originated in China during the Han dynasty. Simplified Chinese was adapted in the 1950s from the traditional set of Han ideographs and is widely used in the People's Republic of China (PRC) and in Southeast Asia, including Singapore. Taiwan and Hong Kong prefer traditional Chinese. In both simplified and traditional Chinese, an ideograph usually consists of two or more parts: one part generally represents meaning, and the other represents pronunciation. Occasionally, both parts represent meaning. The radical is the most important element. It categorizes an ideograph with respect to its meaning and is sometimes compared to the concept of a word root in English. Ideographs are traditionally arranged by their radicals, of which there are several hundred.

To complicate matters, vertical writing is commonly used for some East Asian writing systems, such as Japanese or Chinese. Lines of text are drawn top to bottom and flow from right to left. Although ideographic characters are shown upright, other characters are typically rotated 90 degrees. However, it should also be mentioned that the number of ideographs needed for everyday use by Japanese, Korean, and Chinese people is relatively small compared to the huge set of ideographs available. In addition, an identical subset of ideographs occurs in Japanese, Korean, and simplified and traditional Chinese.

Yet another complication is that writing systems have evolved to be either unidirectional or bidirectional (bi di). Unidirectional systems write on lines uniformly from left to right or from top to bottom. Chinese, Japanese, and Korean are considered unidirectional systems. Although they may mix vertical and horizontal writing on the same page, they never mix two directions of writing in a single line. Arabic and Hebrew, on the other hand, allow writing in different directions, such as text from right to left and numbers and interspersed words from Roman scripts from left to right. On pages written in a bidirectional language, the text starts in the upper right corner, as do the graphics.

In addition, in the Arabic system characters are context sensitive (i.e., dependent on the surrounding characters). The characters are written differently depending on whether the character is at the beginning, middle, or end of a word or if it is used by itself (referred to as initial, median, final, or isolated). As a result, when Arabic text is typed, previously entered characters change in appearance. Then there are languages like Thai, which use a relatively small number of letters but cluster them in words with multiple marks stacked above them. A Thai character can be thought of as a column position on a display screen with four display cells. Each column position can have up to three characters. The composition of a display cell is based on the character's classification. Some Thai characters can be composed with another character's classification. If they can be composed together, both characters will be in the same cell. Otherwise, they will be in separate cells. Thai, like such languages as Farsi and Urdu, which have long ascenders and descenders, takes up more room for display and printing.

HOW CAN A COMPUTER HANDLE
ALL OF THESE WRITING SYSTEMS?

Human beings understand symbols, such as letters, digits, punctuation, and so on, while computers like to deal with numbers. A computer stores and reproduces text by assigning numbers in its memory to represent glyphs. A glyph can be a letter, number, symbol, or ideograph from any writing system. Once mapped, the association between a glyph and its number is known as a character or code point.[1] It is important to understand that the term *character* in this context refers to the abstract meaning of a particular shape. The character or code point is used to represent the character's location in a particular place in the text without indicating anything about its actual shape, size, color, and so forth. A font handles the visual representation of the character. The resulting set of numbers (after a language has been mapped) is called a character set.

Encoding is the way in which the character set (made up of the numbers or code points) is converted into a sequence of bytes and stored in the computer's memory. A computer's memory is structured into units known as bytes. Each byte or unit is made up of a collection of bits. A bit, or binary digit, is the smallest piece of data that a computer recognizes and is represented by the presence or absence of an electronic pulse, a 0 or 1. The length of a byte or unit of memory was set originally as 7 bits (for example 0001110 or 1100010). As a result, one unit or byte could store or encode 128 different characters (2^7). This encoding scheme was called the American Standard Code for Information Interchange (ASCII). The size of the byte was later increased to 8 bits, and thus, 256 different characters could be encoded (2^8).[2]

For alphabet-based languages like English, French, and most Western European languages, the extended ASCII encoding system using one byte of memory was sufficient for what is known as the Latin-1 character set (standardized by the International Organization for Standardization (ISO) as ISO-8859-1). In these languages it is possible to use fewer than 256 symbols (A–Z lower/upper case, 0–9, and accents) to create thousands of words. Languages like Japanese, Korean, and Chinese, however, have more than 256 symbols. Character sets capable of handling thousands of symbols had to be developed for ideographic languages. These character sets cannot be accommodated in 256 code points (or one byte); they have to be encoded using two bytes. Two bytes provide for the possibility of storing up to 65,536 glyphs (256 × 256). Table 2.1 lists a few of the main character sets.

Table 2.1   Examples of Character Sets

ISO-8859-1 or CP-1252 or Latin-1	Western European
ISO-8859-2 or CP-1250 or Latin-2	Eastern European
ISO-8859-3	Esperanto, Galician, Maltese
ISO-8859-5, KO18-R	Cyrillic
ISO-8859-6	Arabic
ISO-8859-7 or CP-1253	Greek
ISO-8859-8	Hebrew
ISO-8859-9	Turkish
ISO-8859-10	Scandinavian, Baltic
GB2312, GB18030-2000 (can hold 1.6 million characters)	Simplified Chinese
Big5, EUC-TW	Traditional Chinese
Shift_JIS, EUC-JP	Japanese
ISO-2022-KR, EUC-KR	Korean

Mixing character sets on the same web page, however, was difficult. Look-up tables were needed for computers to talk to each other and to transfer text. Every piece of textual data had to be tagged with a character set, and data was often corrupted if text from different character sets was mixed. In essence, web designers were forced into monolingual pages. The solution was Unicode.

UNDERSTANDING UNICODE

The Unicode Standard is a character coding system designed to support the worldwide interchange, processing, and display of the written texts of the diverse languages of the modern world. In addition, it supports classical and historical texts of many written languages.[3]

Historically, two different groups set out to assign each glyph in the world a number and thus create a multilingual character set that could accommodate all the letters, punctuation, and technical symbols in common use in different languages. One group was the ISO 10646 project of the International Organization of Standardization, which worked on the Universal Character Set (UCS); the other was the Unicode Project organized by a consortium of manufacturers of multilingual software. The two groups began to work together in 1991. Although both groups publish their individual standards independently, they have agreed to keep the code tables of the Unicode Standard and the Universal Character Set compatible with each other. The HTML 4.01 Specification has also adopted the UCS—and thus the Unicode Standard—as a character set for HTML.

The current version (3.2) of the Unicode Standard,[4] developed by the Unicode Consortium, assigns a unique identifier to each of 94,140 glyphs. These glyphs cover the world's principal written languages and many mathematical and other symbols. The character sets of many currently existing international, national, and corporate standards are also incorporated in the Unicode Standard. For example, the first 256 characters are taken from the Latin-1 character set (which covers Western European languages).

There are three key things to remember about Unicode:

1. Unicode is language-independent. A character *b* can be a French, German, or English *b*, even if it has different meanings

in the different languages. In the same way, a particular Han ideograph might map to a character used in Chinese Hanzi, Japanese Kanji, or Korean Hanja.

2. Unicode has nothing to do with the appearance of the language, which is determined by the fonts used. In combination with the correct fonts, however, Unicode can be used to represent several languages, using different alphabets or ideographs, on the same web page.

3. Unicode is a character set. The Unicode code points have to be encoded or turned into a sequence of bytes, as discussed above. There are currently three different encodings in existence: UTF-8, UTF-16, and UTF-32.[5] All three encoding forms can, if need be, use 4 bytes (or 32 bits) of data for each character. UTF-8 is the encoding used on the web. It can work out which values in a text string are single byte codes (typically alphabetic languages) and which are double byte codes (typically ideographic languages).

The Unicode standard has become especially important for library automation as libraries accommodate foreign-based materials and work with multicultural patrons. The library automation products that incorporate Unicode capabilities can expand their applications not only to a variety of countries but also to include more diverse collections, regardless of language or source. For a list of library automation vendors and Unicode compliance, see appendix A.

While the existence—and continued development—of Unicode has made possible a multilingual web, it is, of course, a work in progress. Suzanne Topping discusses some ongoing issues in her May 2001 article.[6]

PUTTING IT ALL TOGETHER ON A WEB PAGE

Based on the discussion above, the website designer must consider the following when designing web pages for a multinational audience:

- The web page must be presented in the correct character set, or the content of the page will appear as a jumble of meaningless symbols.
- The web page must be delivered in the desired natural language (Swedish, English, etc.,) and dialect (U.S., British, etc.).

- The web page must be presented in the correct directionality.
- The user must have or be able to access the correct fonts.

Ensuring the Correct Character Set

The Internet is based on a client–server relationship. The server, sometimes thought of as the printing press of the digital age, contains content. The client (the browser) accesses the server and requests information from the server software. The process is managed by the Hypertext Transfer Protocol (HTTP). The HTTP protocol, or set of rules, enables the client to make requests and the server to reply by returning the requested documents (web pages), along with sufficient information for the client to interpret them correctly.

Clearly, among the most important information that must be requested and returned is the character set. The most effective way to ensure that the correct character set is used is to code the information into the pages' meta tags, particularly by using the meta tag attribute http-equiv. Http-equiv can take a value of content-type with a parameter of content, which tells the client browser what kind of data the server is sending: HTML text, plain text, gif images, mpeg sounds, and so on. Content-type can also take a parameter called charset (short for character set). The value of the charset parameter should be determined by your design. If you have different languages on a single page, then the charset should be set to UTF-8 (Unicode). For example:

```
<meta http-equiv="content-type"
content="text/html;charset=UTF-8" />
```

If you have individual pages that are purely in a particular language, you can also set the charset on every page to UTF-8 (Unicode). However, you might want to consider setting the charset very specifically for the particular language to be absolutely sure that the user receives the pages in the correct format. For example, for Japanese pages, the charset instruction might read as follows:

```
<meta http-equiv="content-type"
content="text/html;charset=Shift_JIS" />
```

The traditional Chinese page charset instruction might read as follows:

```
<meta http-equiv="content-type"
content="text/html;charset=Big5" />.
```

And the simplified Chinese page charset instruction might read as follows:

```
<meta http-equiv="content-type"
content="text/html;charset=GB2312" />.
```

Examples of setting specific charsets can be found at the Symantec website for the pages in Korean, traditional Chinese, simplified Chinese, and Japanese.[7] The United Nations website also uses specific charsets for its pages in Arabic, simplified Chinese, French, Russian, and Spanish.[8]

Character encoding is equally important if you are using forms on a multilingual web page. If the charset does not have a value of UTF-8, characters input into form elements (such as text or text area input boxes) will not get converted to UTF-8; they will remain in the standard encoding as set in the client browser, and the resulting information will be meaningless. Sorting is another reason for making sure that your multilingual web page is encoded as UTF-8. Sort order is not the same for all languages (see table 2.2). In English sorting is typically done from *a* to *z*. In Danish the letter *z* sorts before other letters. It is not the last letter of the alphabet. In Danish and Norwegian *ae* comes after *z*, *o* after *ae*, and *ä* after *o*. In German, characters with an umlaut (two dots on top

Table 2.2   Sorting and Collating Sequences

American: cg<ch<ci; lk<ll<lm; rq<rr<rs
Spanish: cz<ch<d; lz<ll<m; rz<rr<s
French: e<ë<ê<é<è
German: sr<ß<st
Danish: Z<Æ<Ø<Å
Dutch: IJ = Y or = "IJ"

of a vowel) sort directly after the character without an umlaut. Germans treat *ue* and *ae* as equivalent to *ü* or *ä*. In German β is one character, but it is treated as a double character and is the equivalent of *ss*. The Spanish *ch* is a double character that is treated as a separate single character and is ordered after *c* and before *d*. But in the middle of a word, it comes after the dual character *cz* and before the single character *d*. The Spanish double character *ll* is also treated as a separate single character and is ordered after *l* and before *m*. But in the middle of a word it comes after the dual character *lz* and before the single character *m*. Also in Spanish *ñ* is a separate letter sorted after *n* and before *o*. In many Asian cultures, ideographs are put together by a prescribed tradition of brushstrokes and sorted by the brush stroke order. A user might want to sort Chinese ideographs by the number of strokes required to represent the ideograph, the radical (root) of the ideograph, or the number of strokes added to the radical.

Language

Language can also be specified in the meta tags using http-equiv. For example:

```
<meta http-equiv="content-language" content="en" />
```

A number of languages can be specified in this way:

```
<meta http-equiv="content-language"
content="en,ar,fr,vi" />
```

You can also add information:

```
<meta name="language" content="Deutsch, de" />
```

This statement (meta name = "language") should not replace the meta http-equiv="content-language" statement, which helps the browser communicate with the server software and may direct or control how the web page will be displayed. The meta name="language" only provides informational data for robots and search engines.

In the case of language, however, it is better to use the lang attribute introduced in HTML 4.0[9] because it will give you greater control. If the entire document is in the same language, you can put the lang attribute in the html tag or element. The value is made up of a two-letter language code with an optional specification for a country or a dialect. For example:

```
<html lang="en"> for English
<html lang="es"> for Spanish
<html lang="en-us"> for American English
<html lang="fr"> for French
<html lang=" zh_cn "> for simplified Chinese used
in mainland China
<html lang=" zh_hk "> for traditional Chinese used
in Hong Kong
<html lang=" zh_3G "> for simplified Chinese used
in Singapore
<html lang=" zh_tw "> for traditional Chinese used
in Taiwan
```

The list of language codes is based on ISO 639.[10] Codes can be accessed by their English name or by their bibliographic or terminology code. The ISO 639-2 Registration Authority in the United States is the Library of Congress, which is slowly adding codes for a variety of dialects.[11]

The lang attribute can also be used with most tags or elements. To switch languages within a document, place a lang attribute within the appropriate tag or element. As discussed in chapter 5, XHTML prefers the addition of xml: lang ="xx" as well as lang ="xx." For example:

```
<p xml:lang = "fr" lang="fr"> French paragraph</p>
<p xml:lang = "en" lang="en"> English text....
<span xml:lang = "es" lang="es"> some Spanish
text</span>
English text continues...</p>
```

A tag or element inherits language-code information following an order of precedence with the html tag being the highest order. In the following example, the primary language of the page is English (en). One paragraph is declared to be in Spanish (es), after which the primary language returns to English. The next paragraph includes an embedded Japanese (ja) phrase, after which the primary language returns to English.

```
<!DOCTYPE html PUBLIC "-//W3C//DTD XHTML 1.0
Transitional//EN""http://www.w3.org/TR/xhtml1/DTD/
xhtml1-transitional.dtd">
<html xml:lang = "en" lang="en">
<head>
<meta http-equiv="content-type"
content="text/html; charset=UTF-8" />
</head>
<body>
English...
<p xml:lang ="es" lang="es"> Spanish...</p>
<p>English again...</p>
<p>English with <em xml:lang= "ja" lang="ja"> some
Japanese </em>English begins here again...</p>
</body>
</html>
```

Content Negotiation

Another way to handle multiple languages on a web page is by means of content negotiation. Content negotiation is where a message is sent to the server software by the browser indicating in which language(s) the browser wants to receive web pages. This is typically a prioritized list, and the server software automatically selects the correct document in the correct language (assuming, of course, that web pages written in different languages are stored on the server). How does content negotiation work?

The HTTP standard includes an *Accept-Language* header that the client browser can send to the server as part of a request for a web page. Both Internet Explorer and Netscape allow users to set an *Accept-Language* header by specifying their preferred languages or locale, in order of preference. If, for example, a user selected French (language) and British English (locale), the *Accept-Language* header might look as follows:

```
Accept-Language: fr, en-gb
```

This header specifies that French is the preferred language, followed by British English. The server software would then send the French-language page, and if that did not exist, it would send the British English–language page.

The *Accept-Language* header in the Internet Explorer browser is set as follows:

1. In Internet Explorer, click the *Tools* menu.
2. Click *Internet Options*.
3. On the *General* tab, click the *Languages* button.
4. Select the language you want, and then use the *Move Up* button to place your selection at the top of the list of languages. Click *OK*. Notice the *Add* button, which enables you to add languages.
5. Click *OK* in the *Internet Options* dialog box and restart the browser (see figure 2.1).

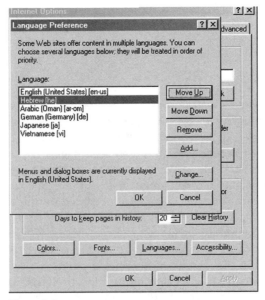

Figure 2.1

The problem with this solution is that it only works if the server software has been set up to recognize the *Accept-Language* header. You have to configure the server software to allow document language selection in accordance with the preferences indicated by the browser. One of the most popular server software programs, Apache, can handle content negotiation, including language selection.[12] However, not all server software has this capability. Also, the user will have to make the changes in his or her browser, then undo them on visiting other multilingual sites. Because as little as possible should be required from the user, it is best to try to control the language presentation from the code on the web page as discussed above.

Cookies

Another option for controlling language is to use cookies, which are small computer-generated text files that are sent to the user's computer. They store information on that computer for retrieval in later browsing sessions. The first time a user visits a site, he or she will be prompted to select a language from a list. This causes a cookie to be stored on the user's local computer and sent by the user's browser back to the server on every subsequent request. However, if a user moves to a different computer or deletes the cookie file, the language preference will be lost. This technique will be discussed in chapter 6, but once again, it seems best to control language from the coding on the web page(s).

Directionality

Since the creation of HTML 4.0, the webpage designer can specify the directionality of the text by use of the dir attribute,[13] which takes a value of ltr (left-to-right) or rtl (right-to-left). The default is ltr. If the whole page is in one language, the attribute can go in the html tag. For example:

```
<!DOCTYPE html PUBLIC "-//W3C//DTD XHTML 1.0
Transitional//EN" "http://www.w3.org/TR/xhtml1/DTD/
xhtml1-transitional.dtd">
<html xml:lang = "en" lang="en" dir="ltr">
```
                                       continued on next page

```
<head>
<meta http-equiv="content-type"
content="text/html; charset=UTF-8" />
<meta http-equiv="keywords" content="an
appropriate list of words" />
<meta name="author" content="My Name" />
<title>A Sample Page</title>
</head>
<body>
........
</body>
</html>
```

The lang and dir attributes can be used with other tags or elements in the body to enable different languages to be used on the same page. In the following example, the primary text direction for the entire web page is set in the html tag or element. Direction is changed for other languages as necessary.

```
<!DOCTYPE html PUBLIC "-//W3C//DTD XHTML 1.0
Transitional//EN""http://www.w3.org/TR/xhtml1/DTD/
xhtml1-transitional.dtd">
<html xml: lang = "en" lang="en" dir="ltr">
<head>
<meta http-equiv="content-type"
content="text/html; charset=UTF-8" />
<meta http-equiv="keywords" content="an
appropriate list of words" />
<meta name="author" content="My Name" />
<title>A Sample Page</title>
</head>
<body>
<p>A paragraph of English text</p>
<p xml:lang = "ar" lang ="ar" dir="rtl">A
paragraph of Arabic text</p>
<p>A further paragraph of English text
<p><q xml:lang = "ar" lang="ar" dir="rtl">An
Arabic quotation</q></p>
</body>
</html>
```

However, consider the following code and its output as a web page (see figure 2.2):

```
<!DOCTYPE html PUBLIC "-//W3C//DTD XHTML 1.0
Transitional//EN""http://www.w3.org/TR/xhtml1/DTD/
xhtml1-transitional.dtd">
<html dir="rtl">
<head>
<meta http-equiv="content-type"
content="text/html; charset=UTF-8" />
<title>My Page</title>
</head>
<body>
...right-to-left text...
<p dir="ltr">...left-to-right text...</p>
<p>...right-to-left text again...</p>
</body>
</html>
```

...right-to-left text...

...left-to-right text...

...right-to-left text again...

Figure 2.2

The direction is set in the html tag as right-to-left. However, note that this causes characters to start on the right and move left. It does not affect the direction of the actual letters because directionality is implicit in the text. The characters are implicitly left-to-right.

If you want to display a mixture of left-to-right and right-to-left characters in a single direction, you can override the intrinsic directional properties of the characters by using the bidirectional override, or bdo, tag or element. It is important to remember to set an initial text direction. For example:

```
<!DOCTYPE html PUBLIC "-//W3C//DTD XHTML 1.0
Transitional//EN""http://www.w3.org/TR/xhtml1/DTD/
xhtml1-transitional.dtd">
<html xml:lang = "en" lang = "en" dir="ltr">
```
continued on next page

```
<head>
<meta http-equiv="content-type"
content="text/html; charset=UTF-8" />
<title>My Page</title>
</head>
<body>
<p>an English paragraph</p>
<p xml:lang = "he" lang = "he"
dir = "rtl"><bdo>Hebrew text</bdo></p>
<p>This is another English paragraph</p>
</body>
</html>
```

Figure 2.3 shows a page produced by this coding. Note that Netscape (as of version 6.1) does not handle the bdo tag or element. It is actually best to control direction by means of a stylesheet as discussed in chapter 5.

an English paragraph

txet werbeH

This is another English paragraph

Figure 2.3

Understanding the Importance of Fonts

In addition to the correct encoding, the reader of the web page must have the appropriate fonts installed for a page to display correctly. This becomes especially crucial with Chinese, Japanese, and Korean (CJK) languages. As discussed above, Unicode provides one code point for each Han character. However, the display of the same Han character is different in traditional Chinese, simplified Chinese, Japanese, and Korean. For example, the traditional Chinese glyph for *grass* uses four strokes for the grass radical, whereas the simplified Chinese, Japanese, and Korean glyphs use three. It is the appropriate font that provides the appropriate visual representation of the character in each language.

If the webpage designer sets the charset and the language attribute(s) in the web pages as discussed above, Internet Explorer will be able to download and install the correct fonts on the user's computer automatically (see figure 2.4). For example, when faced with a Web page in Hebrew, Internet Explorer will offer to download the Miriam font; when faced with simplified Chinese, it will offer to download MS Hei or MS Song; and when faced with traditional Chinese, it will offer to download MingLiu.

Figure 2.4

Embedded Fonts

What if you are using a language that requires very special fonts? You can try embedding the fonts in the web page so that your user has minimal trouble. An embedded font is used temporarily by a web browser and then discarded after the user is done with that web page. When you embed a font, you can specify the exact web pages on which it will work. Steve Mulder has an excellent tutorial on embedding fonts on the Webmonkey site.[14] As with setting charset and language, it is advisable to control fonts explicitly via the web page coding. The most efficient way to do this is by using a stylesheet as discussed in chapter 5.

CONFIGURING PUBLIC WORKSTATIONS

The following instructions recommend the best way to set up public Internet workstations in public libraries. Depending on your user base, it might be useful to make these instructions available to users so that they can configure their browsers in an optimum fashion at home. The instructions—designed as graphics—could be provided in various target languages. This is discussed in chapter 6 in the section entitled "Turning Text into Graphics."

Internet Explorer Browser Configuration

When installing Internet Explorer (IE), select the customized installation option (*Install Minimal*) (see figure 2.5). Then, select multilanguage support, language autoselection, text-display support, and text-input support for as many languages as you wish (see figure 2.6). At present, Japanese, Korean, Pan-European, traditional Chinese, simplified Chinese, Vietnamese, Hebrew, Arabic, and Thai are listed.

If IE is already installed and you do not wish to reinstall but want to make sure that the correct fonts are loaded, do the following:

Connect to the Internet.
Select *View/Encoding/More*.

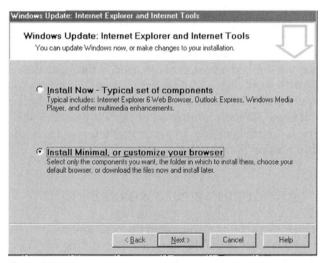

Figure 2.5

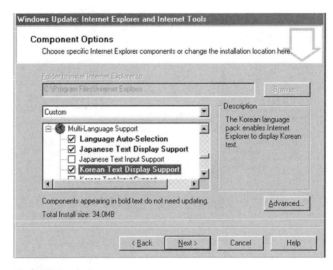

Figure 2.6

Select the language(s) you want (see figure 2.7). If the fonts are not on the computer, Internet Explorer will automatically download and install the correct fonts for you. Once the fonts are downloaded they will work with any browser.

In either case (installing from scratch or adding fonts), finish up by selecting *View/Encoding/Auto-Select* or *View/Encoding/Unicode (UTF-8)* (see figure 2.8).

If you wish to change the language of menus and dialog boxes on the browser, do the following (see figure 2.9):

Select *Tools/Internet Options/General/Languages.*
Select *Change.*
Select *Add* to connect to Microsoft's site to add interfaces in other languages. You will be taken to the Microsoft Windows Update page. Look for *International Language Support.* The direct link is windowsupdate.microsoft.com/default.htm?page=productupdates.

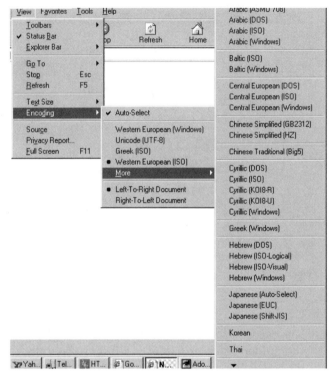

Figure 2.7

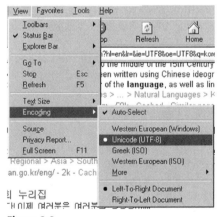

Figure 2.8

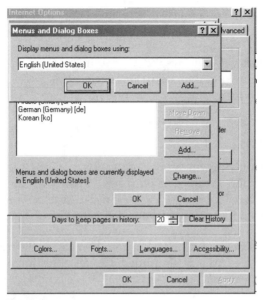

Figure 2.9

Tango Browser

The Tango multilingual web browser was developed by Alis Technologies. It has a multilingual interface (but does not translate material). It lets the user switch into different languages, select a correct charset, and change the direction of the text. The keyboard layout can also be switched (see the discussion in chapter 4). Tango Professional handled 19 languages. Unfortunately, only Tango Lite (which is limited to English, French, and Arabic) is still available.[15] The Tango browser was an ideal solution for public workstations in libraries serving multilingual patrons. The New York Public Library used Tango in several of its branches.[16] Instructions to users are presented using text as graphics (as discussed in chapter 6).

An excellent resource for obtaining information on customizing browsers can be found at Unicode Resources: "Unicode and Multilingual Web Browsers," a site maintained by Alan Wood.[17] Yale University Library has some useful information on its website covering multilanguage support in the Yale library and the appropriate configuration of browsers.[18] The following test pages are helpful for checking out how well a browser is handling a particular language:

www.library.yale.edu/wsg/docs/multilanguage/samples.htm
www.unicode.org/iuc/iuc10/languages.html
www.unicode.org/iuc/iuc10/x-utf8.html

Unicode Fonts

If you can only download one or two fonts, it is best to install Unicode fonts like Arial Unicode MS, Bitstream CyberBit, and Code2000.[19] Arial Unicode MS can handle Arabic, Armenian, Bengali, simplified Chinese, traditional Chinese, Devanagari, Georgian, Gujarati, Gumukhi, Japanese, Kannada, Korean, Malayan, Orriya, Tamil, Thai, Tibetan, and most Western languages. Bitstream CyberBit can handle Arabic, simplified Chinese, traditional Chinese, Japanese, Korean, and Thai.

NOTES

1. Sometimes also called a *scalar value*.
2. Known as extended ASCII.
3. "The Unicode Standard" at www.unicode.org/unicode/standard/standard.html (accessed March 1, 2002).
4. "Unicode Home Page" at www.unicode.org (accessed March 1, 2002).
5. UTF stands for Unicode Transformation Format.
6. Suzanne Topping, "The Secret Life of Unicode: A Peek at Unicode's Soft Underbelly," May 2001, at www-106.ibm.com/developerworks/unicode/library/u-secret.html (accessed March 1, 2002).
7. See www.symantec.com/region/kr; www.symantec.com/region/tw; www.symantec.com/region/cn; www.symantec.com/region/jp.
8. See www.un.org/arabic; www.un.org/chinese; www.un.org/french; www.un.org/russian; www.un.org/spanish.
9. "Tags for the Identification of Language" at www.ietf.org/rfc/rfc3066.txt (accessed March 1, 2002).
10. "Codes for the Representation of Names of Languages" at lcweb.loc.gov/standards/iso639-2/langhome.html (accessed March 1, 2002).
11. "Registration Authority: ISO 639-2" at www.loc.gov/standards/iso639-2 (accessed March 1, 2002).

12. "Apache HTTP Server Project" at httpd.apache.org (accessed March 1, 2002); "Apache HTTP Server: Content Negotiation" at http.apache.org/docs/content-negotiation.html (accessed March 1, 2002).

13. Do not confuse the dir attribute with the dir tag or element. The dir tag or element is used with li (list) to create a directory list. The tag was depreciated in HTML 4.0.

14. Steve Mulder, "Embedding Fonts Tutorial" at hotwired.lycos.com/webmonkey/design/fonts/tutorials/tutorial2.html (accessed March 1, 2002).

15. See www.translation.net/tango.html; www.worldlanguage.com.

16. New York Public Library, "Browsing the Web in Many Languages Using Tango" at www.nypl.org/branch/multi/help.htm (accessed March 1, 2002).

17. Alan Wood, "Unicode Resources: Unicode and Multilingual Web Browsers" at www.alanwood.net/unicode/browsers.html (accessed March 1, 2002).

18. "IE 5.5 and Netscape 6 Setup: Multilanguage Support in the Yale Library" at www.library.yale.edu/~lso/workstation/docs/multilanguage/multilanguage.html (accessed March 1, 2002).

19. "Arial Unicode MS" at www.alanwood.net/unicode/fonts.html#arialunicodems (accessed March 1, 2002); "Code2000" at www.alanwood.net/unicode/fonts.html#code2000 (accessed March 1, 2002).

REFERENCES

Davis, Mark. "Forms of Unicode," 1999, at www.106.ibm.com/developerworks/library/utfencodingforms/index.html (accessed March 1, 2002).

Graham, Tony. *Unicode: A Primer.* Foster City, Calif.: Hungry Minds, 2000.

Ishida, Richard. "Non-Latin Script Characteristics" at www.xeroxemea.com/globaldesign/free.htm#scripts (accessed March 1, 2002).

Korpela, Jukka. " A Tutorial on Character Code Issues," 2001, at www.malibutelecom.com/yucca/chars.html (accessed March 1, 2002).

Lunde, Ken, and Gigi Estabrooke. *CJKV Information Processing.* Beijing: O'Reilly, 1999.

MSDN Library. "Character Set Recognition" at msdn.microsoft.com/library/default.asp?url=/workshop/author/dhtml/reference/charsets/charset4.asp (accessed March 1, 2002).

MSDN Library. "HTML Character Sets" at msdn.microsoft.com/library/default.asp?url=/workshop/author/dhtml/reference/charsets/charsets.asp (accessed March 1, 2002).

Pyatt, Elizabeth J. "Techniques and Tips for Foreign Language Web Sites" at ets.cac.psu.edu/users/ejp10/international/tutorial/01/def.html (accessed March 1, 2002).

Searle, Steven. "A Brief History of Character Codes in North America, Europe, and East Asia," 1999, at tronweb.super-nova.co.jp/characcodehist.html (accessed March 1, 2002).

"What is Unicode?" at www.unicode.org/unicode/standard/WhatIs Unicode.html (accessed March 1, 2002).

Wood, Alan. " Unicode Resources, Unicode and Multilingual Support in HTML, Fonts, Web Browsers and Other Applications" at www.alanwood. net/unicode (accessed March 1, 2002).

Yergeau, François, and Martin Durst. "Weaving the Multilingual Web" at www.w3.org/Talks/1999/0830-tutorial-unicode-mjd/ (accessed March 1, 2002).

3

Subjective and Objective Cultural Considerations

Designers and users of websites may have very different cultural backgrounds. Culture can be defined as something that an individual learns while growing up with peers in a community or society. As J. E. Beer points out, culture is grounded in the group experience. It is an individual's sense of identity within the group; it is his or her relationship to other humans, to things, to animals, to gods, and to the cosmos.[1] A culture often contains several subcultures, and cultures overlap.

The website designer must always remember that although he or she is thinking in terms of the global reach of the website, the user is coming to the website from a local perspective. Also, the variety of high-level, easy-to-use authoring tools for building websites makes it easy to create visuals, such as buttons, windows, and scroll boxes. However, the general look and functionality of the website is thus more or less preset and does not take into account the subjective and objective cultural issues specific to target cultures.

SUBJECTIVE CULTURE: MODELS

Subjective culture is psychological and deals with attitudes. Inevitably, researchers and writers have developed different models of and ways of looking at cultures.[2] Geert Hofstede saw culture as the collective mental programming of the people in an environment.[3] People with different mental programming perceive the same object in different ways. Hofstede studied IBM employees in 50 countries and identified the following 5 cultural dimensions that impact work, home and family life, and education and that appear in a nation's or culture's symbols, heroes, rituals, and values:

> Power distance (the measure of inequality in a society and the degree to which people accept that inequality);
> Individualism and collectivism;
> Femininity and masculinity (masculine cultures have social roles clearly defined by gender whereas these roles overlap in feminine societies);
> Uncertainty avoidance (the extent to which members of a culture feel threatened by the unknown);
> Long-term time orientation (how well a culture adapts its traditions to modern perspectives).

Hofstede's model of culture has been criticized for ignoring diversity within national cultures and for viewing the individual as simply the passive recipient of culture.[4] In a 2001 paper, however, Aaron Marcus and Emile W. Gould consider how Hofstede's dimensions of culture might affect user interface designs.[5] They use many examples from the web to illustrate his cultural dimensions. For example, cultures that are high in uncertainty avoidance prefer links that follow a strict sequence. The following briefly illustrates how Hofstede's conclusions can be applied to web pages designed for a Chinese audience.

Impact of Power Distance on Designing Chinese Web Pages

Power distance is the extent to which less powerful members expect and accept unequal power distribution within a culture. Hofstede found that countries like the United States and Britain had a small power distance index and thus favored an egalitarian ethos. Countries with a Chinese majority, or that had undergone Chinese cultural influences, however, had medium to upper-medium power distance indexes. Chinese people therefore "[a]ccept and appreciate inequality but feel that the use of power should be moderated by a sense of obligation."[6] Thus, web pages designed for Chinese users should include references to characteristics associated with large power distance indexes, including the following:

- References to authority, power, expertise, and wealth;
- A strong focus on expertise, authority, official stamps, and logos;

- Prominent organizational charts that emphasize the organization's hierarchy;
- Clear statement of any special titles that have been conferred on members of the organization so that they can be properly addressed;
- Significant or frequent emphasis on the social and moral order (e.g., nationalism and government leaders) and its symbols.

Impact of Collectivism on Designing Chinese Web Pages

> Individualistic societies expect individuals to look after themselves and their immediate families, while people in collectivist societies are organized into strong, cohesive in-groups which support them (and which they support) throughout their lives.[7]

Hofstede found American society to have the highest level of individualism among the 50 countries that he studied. Individualistic cultures value freedom and material rewards at work and are very direct in business communications. Hofstede considered the Chinese to be collectivist in nature. Collectivist cultures value harmony, and their business communications are much less direct than those of more individualistic cultures. Since the Chinese culture is a collectivist one, web pages designed for Chinese users should do the following:

- Place little emphasis on personal achievement;
- Define success in terms of sociopolitical, rather than individual, goals;
- Promote group solidarity rather than individual self-interest;
- Include links to other organizations to illustrate a strong group network;
- Be written in an indirect, impersonal style;
- Emphasize tradition and history.

Impact of Masculinity versus Femininity on Designing Chinese Web Pages

Masculine cultures have clearly distinct social gender roles, while these roles overlap in feminine cultures. Hofstede's study did not explicitly mention China's masculinity index. According to ITIM Culture and Management Consultants, however, China has a medium masculinity index slightly lower than that of the United States.[8] As a result, a website localized for Chinese users does not require any of the design features advisable for either very masculine or very feminine societies.

Impact of Low Uncertainty Avoidance on Designing Chinese Web Pages

Uncertainty avoidance reflects the extent to which members of a culture feel threatened by the unknown. China, Chinese-speaking countries, and countries whose population includes a sizeable Chinese minority have a low uncertainty avoidance. Marcus and Gould[9] recommend that websites designed for users from low-uncertainty avoidance cultures, such as the Chinese cultures, should include the following:

- Many choices and a large amount of information;
- Minimal control over the user's navigation around the site with an emphasis on encouraging wandering by the user.

Impact of Long-Term Time Orientation on Designing Chinese Web Pages

Hofstede found China to have the highest long-term orientation index of all the countries he surveyed. A high long-term orientation index indicates that a culture adapts tradition to modern perspectives and displays patience in pursuing goals. Websites aimed at users from cultures with high long-term orientation indexes should therefore emphasize the following:

- Perseverance and patience in pursuing goals;
- Future orientation;
- Content with a practical application;
- Relationships as a source of information.

The model developed by Edward Hall, which has become widely accepted among sociolinguists, can help web designers in understanding what target cultures can and will accept.[10] Hall compares the cultures of the world on a scale ranging from high-context to low-context (see table 3.1). In cultures that are closer to

Table 3.1 Characteristics of High-Context and Low-Context Cultures

High-Context Culture	Low-Context Culture
Implicit messages	Explicit messages
Internalized messages	Plainly coded messages
Nonverbal coding	Verbalized details
Reserved reactions	Reactions on the surface
Distinct in-groups and out-groups	Flexible in-groups and out-groups
Strong people bonds	Fragile people bonds
High commitment	Low commitment
Open and flexible time	Highly organized time

the high-context end of the scale, important information is transmitted in nonverbal or indirect ways. Meaning is implied. Nothing is expressed directly; body language, tone, the status of individuals, and pauses and silences are important. Group-oriented cultures, such as the Chinese, Japanese, Korean, Latin American, Mediterranean, Middle Eastern, and Vietnamese cultures, tend to fall into this category. France also places close to the high-context end of the scale. In cultures that are closer to the low-context end of the scale, virtually all information is communicated with a direct statement. People say what they mean. In low-context cultures, the individual takes precedence over the group. Countries that place closer to this end of the scale include the United States, Canada, the United Kingdom, Australia, Germany, and most of Western Europe, including Scandinavia. Following Hall's theories web pages designed for a Chinese audience should focus on the following:

- Communications that rely on highly developed personal relationships rather than detailed facts and agreements;
- Providing a variety of views and topics;
- An orientation toward people rather than tasks.

Yvonne Cleary examines the role of subjective cultural issues on the usability of the Louvre Museum official website.[11]

Subjective Culture: Some Things to Consider

The website designer should avoid jargon, slang, idioms, religion, race, sex, politics, stereotypes, humanized animals, humor, and references to parts of the body. It is important to state what something is rather than what it is called (e.g., use the term *stock exchange* not *Dow*). Use visual images, but remember that not everybody reads from left to right, so the sequencing should be appropriate for the target culture. In particular, remember that humor is very culture specific. What is funny in one culture may not be readily understood in another culture or, worse, may be offensive.

At a minimum the following should be considered when putting together a Web page.

Authority

How is status determined? Is age important? Is money?

Colors

The colors of screens and icons can have different cultural implications. In China white is associated with death and red with marriage and festivity. S. W. Chu, however, observes that red and white are often used together in Chinese society.[12] He argues that Chinese users only find the use of the color white on a website unappealing or inappropriate if it is used in images of people holding white flowers or wearing white clothes. The Japanese also connect white with death, but red spells danger in Japan. In Western Europe, black is associated with death, white with purity and virtue, and red with danger. Western Europeans associate yellow with caution or cowardice, but in Arab countries, yellow signifies happiness. While the color green is acceptable to a Chinese audience, an image of a green hat is not because the expression *wearing a green hat* is used in China to refer to a man who is a cuckold. In Arab countries, green is a holy color. Phrases such as *in the red* or *in the black* may not be understood in cultures that do not use colors as adjectives.

Holzschlag suggests that blue is the most globally accessible color, safe in almost any culture, and it is therefore the best choice for a site being designed for a worldwide audience.[13] A study of international students by Elke Duncker, Yin Leng Theng, and Norlisa Mohd-Nasir reported that European and U.S. students more or less preferred a bright background, black text, and few moderately colorful objects. English students liked pastel color schemes with a lot of gray and low contrast. Scandinavian students tended to prefer dark colors, also with low contrast. Students with a Jamaican background preferred strong and bright colors with high contrasts. African students preferred black as the ground color. No particular pattern seemed to emerge in the use of colors by Asian students. A second survey later in the semester showed that students' color preferences were also affected by the degree of cultural mixing between the country of origin and the local (sub)cultures.[14]

Gestures

How do people stand when they talk to each other? Which hand gestures are acceptable or unacceptable? The "OK" hand gesture is often used as an icon in the United States. In many countries it carries the same meaning as the middle-finger gesture in the United States.

Individuality

Some cultures embrace individuality; others find it offensive.

Learning Styles

Should the style be chatty and friendly or formal, instructional, and scholarly? If the style is informal, will the website be viewed as insulting to users accustomed to receiving a certain amount of respect? There are many studies on different learning styles in different cultures. R. Kaplan noted different organizational styles in English prose written by native speakers of French, Arabic, English, and the Asian languages.[15] J. M. Ulijn found that Dutch readers preferred a direct linear organization, whereas French readers preferred a more digressive organization.[16] In a 1991 study, R. G. Hein found that German readers liked background information giving historical and contextual perspectives. They wanted to see how something fits into the overall scheme of things, and above all they wanted precise information.[17] B. L. Thatcher came to similar conclusions in a 1999 study of South American accountants. The participants in this study wanted contextual and historical information and detailed narratives, which was interesting, as South Americans are regarded as a high-context culture on Hall's scale.[18] Hinds,[19] Maynard,[20] and Kamimura and Oi[21] have found Japanese writing to be inductively organized, with the topic statements appearing late in the text. One study[22] did contradict this and found that if the topic is factual, Japanese readers prefer writing to be deductively organized.[23]

Prejudices

Is there racial equality in the culture? What is considered beautiful or ugly? What are the attitudes toward aging, leisure time, and outsiders?

Roles of Men, Women, and Children

Are the sexes considered equal? How is sexuality treated? Are families large and extended or small and nuclear? Should graphics take into account a disparity between gender roles?

Sense of Time

Is time considered linear and critical or elastic and unimportant relative to other things? The phrase "as soon as possible" means "immediately" in the United States; it often means "when convenient" in other cultures.

Sounds

If using sounds, it is important to remember that telephones, alarms, and sirens sound different in different countries. Also some cultures, such as the Japanese, dislike the use of sounds to correct a user's error.

Symbols

Do shapes, numbers, animals, or food carry meaning? For example, chopsticks in a rice bowl signify the Cantonese symbol of death. The significance of a shamrock as a good luck charm is lost on most non-Western cultures. Thirteen is considered unlucky in the West; four is considered unlucky in Asia, but eight is very lucky. A piggy bank illustrates savings in most parts of the western world. There are, however, countries where pigs are considered unclean. In the United States, a mailbox with a flag is often used to indicate that there is new mail. Mailboxes look different elsewhere. A better symbol would be an envelope. Similarly, the American shopping cart icon for e-commerce does not translate well because in many other countries shoppers use baskets, not carts.

Taboos

Are there religious principles pertaining to certain foods, colors, or behaviors that cannot be violated? What are the culture's attitudes toward body parts? For example, the left hand is offensive in some cultures, so it is better to say "on the left hand" or "left side." Eyes and feet should be avoided as they have negative significance in many cultures.

OBJECTIVE CULTURE

Objective culture is visible. Examples of objective culture are the different ways in which the date, calendars, time, currency, numbers, units of measurement, addresses, and phone numbers are handled around the world. Some efforts have been made to develop universal pictograms and international signage, but in reality there is no globally accepted standard.[24]

Objective Culture: Some Things to Consider

Addresses

Address formats differ from country to country. In many countries the postal code includes letters as well as numbers. Some countries add a country or region code in front of the postal code. Some examples follow:

China
Country
Province City
Address
Last Name   First Name   Honorific

Italy
Street number placed after the street's name: Via Roma 5 bis
Italian postal code before the city: 13034 Cigliano (VC) I (for Italy)

United Kingdom
Postal code after the city or after the country: London PL5 4LZ or London UK S2

Many countries have cities with the same name, so including the country name when listing locations is helpful. If the website uses a form into which visitors can enter names and addresses, the input fields and the programs that process the information should be able to handle various address formats. The order of first and last names varies from culture to culture. For example, a Chinese first name is the family name. In Japan, the surname comes before the given names. A check should be made to determine if the visitor's country or region is either the United States or Canada. Only in those cases should an error message display if the visitor omits the state or province field. Zip codes or postal codes in countries outside of the United States often do not have any particular format or length. An X should not be used to mark a box. Some cultures interpret this as crossing out.

Setting forms up correctly is important especially if you are accepting payments from credit-card holders living outside of the United States. Programming forms with JavaScript is discussed in chapter 6.

Calendars

Many different calendars are in use around the world, such as the Buddhist, Chinese, Gregorian, Hebrew, Hijiri (Middle Eastern), Indian, Islamic, Japanese (Emperor era), Korean (Tangun era), Muslim, and Taiwanese (ROC era), to name a few. In general, many cultures in the West use a Gregorian calendar. Many other cultures, such as Chinese and Japanese, favor a lunar calendar, although they often follow the Gregorian calendar for business and legal purposes. Japan, however, refers to the months in the Gregorian calendar as "first month," "second month," and so on. The Chinese and Japanese lunar calendars (based on the 12-year animal cycle) begin at different times. The Japanese lunar year begins on January 1; the Chinese lunar year typically begins in February. Japan also numbers the years by the reigns of the emperors, with 2002 being Heisei 14 (Heisei 1 started in 1989). Another consideration is that the week starts on Sunday in the United States and on Monday in many other countries.

Currency

There are many different currency units around the world. Table 3.2 gives some examples. Furthermore, local and international symbols for currency can differ. Currency notations can also differ within countries, as is the case in Switzerland (notations vary depending on whether you are dealing with the French-, Italian-, German-, or Romansch-speaking parts of the country) and in Canada (depending on whether you are dealing with the English- or French-speaking parts of the country). Positive and negative currencies are represented differently from country to country and even within the same country. For example:

	Positive	Negative
Norway	kr123,45	kr123,45–
Peru	I/.123,45	I/.–123,45
Portugal	123$45 Esc	–123$45 Esc
South Africa	R123.45	R–123.45
United States	$123.45	($123.45)

It is best to follow standardized international abbreviations as used by the financial world, such as CAD (Canadian dollar), EUR (euro), JPY (Japanese yen), or USD (US dollar). Always explain any abbreviations used on the website. Be aware also that a converted currency amount may take up more or less space than the original amount. To illustrate, USD $1,000 can become 132,769.64 JPY. The web pages should contain a link to a web-based currency converter. Make sure that the currency converter selected has a multilingual interface.

Table 3.2   Some Currencies

Country	Currency	Example
Canada (English)	Dollar ($)	$1 234.56
Canada (French)	Dollar ($)	1 234,56$
Denmark	Kroner (kr)	kr.1.234,56
Japan	Yen	54,284 Yen
Norway	Krone (kr)	kr 1.234,56
Sweden	Krona (Kr)	1234.56KR
Thailand	Baht	2345 Baht
United Kingdom	Pound (£)	45,283.45 pounds
United States	Dollar ($)	$1,234.56

Dates

Date formats are different around the world. The number of digits representing the day, month, or year and the order of the day, month, and year vary significantly from country to country. Even the date separator in the date format varies among different countries, and more than one date separator may be accepted within one country. Table 3.3 lists examples from a selection of countries. Spelling out the date, most notably the month, can help to avoid any confusion that may result from using numerical representations, and always use a four-digit number for the year. A universally understood date format would be January 3rd 2001.

Table 3.3   Some Date Formats

Country	Date Format	Example
Brazil	dd/mm/yy	24/04/01
Bulgaria	yyyy-mm-dd	2001-04-24
Canada (English and French)	yyyy-mm-dd	2001-04-24
Denmark	dd/mm/yy	24/04/01
Finland	dd.mm.yyyy	24.04.2001
France	dd/mm/yy	24/04/01
Germany	dd.mm.yy	24.04.01
Italy	dd.mm.yy	24.04.01
Japan (Gregorian)	yyyy-mm-dd	2001-04-24
Norway	dd.mm.yy	24.04.01
Spain	dd-mm-yy	24-04-01
Sweden	yyyy-mm-dd	2001-04-24
Thailand	dd/mm/yyyy	24/04/2001
United Kingdom	dd/mm/yy	24/04/01
United States	mm-dd-yy	04/24/01

Numbers

If you are using numbers on a website, the coding must allow for different conventions—or for no conventions. Numeric formats vary from country to country, and more than one format may be accepted in one country (e.g., Canada, which has American and French-Canadian numeric notations). Mexico follows the United States with regard to numeric (and calendar) formatting and, thus, differs from the rest of Latin America. The pound sign (#) used as a symbol for number in the United States is rarely used anywhere else in the world. More common is N°.

The United Kingdom and the United States are two of the few places in the world that use a period to indicate the decimal place. Most other countries use a comma. To complicate matters, the United Kingdom and the United States use a comma to separate thousands groups, whereas many other countries use a period, and some countries (e.g., France) use a space. Switzerland uses an apostrophe as a thousand separator; Portugal uses the dollar sign as a decimal separator. A negative number may be denoted by a leading hyphen, a trailing hyphen, or parentheses enclosing the number. For example:

	Positive	*Negative*
United States	12,345.67	–12,345.67
Finland	12 345,67	12 345,67–
Austria	12.345,67	–12.345,67
Canada	12,345.67	–12,345.67
	12 345,67	(12 345,67)
France	12 345,67	–12 345,67
Switzerland	12'345.67	–12'345,67

In addition, rounding of numbers is handled differently in different countries. For example:

United States:
less than or equal to 4: drop digit (123.44 rounds to 123.4)
greater than or equal to 5: add one to previous digit and drop digit (123.46 rounds to 123.5)
Argentina:
less than or equal to 2: change last digit to 0 or drop it (123.452 rounds to 123.45)
less than 8 and greater than 2: change last digit to 5 (123.456 rounds to 123.455)
greater than or equal to 8: add one to second-to-last digit and last digit is 0 or it is dropped (123.459 rounds to 123.46)
Switzerland:
Rounding 12.48 gives 12.50
Rounding 12.523 gives 12.50
Rounding 12.533 gives 12.55
Rounding 12.567 gives 12.55

The words *billion* and *trillion* mean different things in different countries. In the United States, a *billion* means one thousand million; in the

United Kingdom, France, Germany, Italy, and Spain, a *billion* means a million million. In the United States, a *trillion* means one million million; in European countries, it means one million million million.

Phone Numbers

There is no standardization of telephone or fax formats, and each country has its own conventions. For example:

France
Tel. +33 (0) 4-92-95-20-00
    33 1 30 67 28 02
Belgium
    Telefax (32) (4) 344 4335
Hong Kong
Mobile: +852 (9172).8891 Business: +852 2844.1516

Phone number fields in forms should be long enough for any international phone number. In some areas of the world, the local phone number can be 12 digits long. Reserve space for country or region codes and area codes. Use the ISO's recommendation for phone numbers, as follows: +1(408)924-2494

The plus sign represents the international access code that the caller may have to dial first (which he or she will have to locate). The plus sign is followed by the country or region code (*1* stands for the United States and Canada), then the area code, then the local number. References to toll free numbers need to be replaced with the appropriate service in existence in the target country or countries.

Time

Time formats vary around the world. Time can be based on a 12-hour or a 24-hour system. Hour and minute separators are typically either a colon (:) or a period (.). Table 3.4 shows some different time formats. The number of digits representing seconds also varies from country to country. For example:

Austria 22:42:00,030
China (Taiwan): 22:42:00.030
Denmark 22.42.00, 03
Finland 22.42.00, 000

South Africa 22h42:00.030
Switzerland 22, 42, 00
United States 10:42.00 P.M.

Table 3.4 Some Time Formats

Country	Time Format
Canada (English)	8:49 P.M.
Canada (French)	20h49
Finland	20.49
Germany	20.49 Uhr
Norway	Kl 20.49
Thailand	20:49 P.M.
United Kingdom	8.49 p.m. or 20:49

Time zone splits occur between and within countries. Daylight Savings Time (DST) starts and ends on different dates from country to country. The best policy is to standardize to a 24-hour time format (hh:mm:ss). Always include the time zone and explain acronyms, such as Pacific Standard Time (PST) or Central European Time (CET). Include the time difference in terms of how many hours the zone is ahead of, or behind, Greenwich Mean Time (GMT). For example, Office Open 9–18 PST (Pacific Standard Time) (Greenwich Mean Time –8)

The GMT number is not always an integer. Newfoundland, for example, is in a time zone that is half an hour different from the adjacent time zone. Increasingly, the term GMT is being replaced by the term Universal Time (UT) or Universal Time Coordinated (UTC), so the above might also be written as follows: Office Open 9–18 PST (Pacific Standard Time) (Universal Time Coordinated –8)

Units of Measurement

Most parts of the world outside the United States use the metric system[25] as opposed to the Anglo-Saxon or British Imperial system. When designing for international audiences, it is important to provide information in both systems. Temperatures should be provided in both Fahrenheit and centigrade, length in millimeters as well as in inches. For example, Dimensions: 51 × 25 × 76 mm (2" × 1" × 3"). Paper and page also vary in size. Table 3.5 lists some paper sizes.

Table 3.5   Examples of Paper Sizes

Paper Type	Dimensions	Countries
A4	21.0 × 29.7 cm	Everywhere except the United States, Canada, and Japan
A5	14.8 × 21.0 cm	Everywhere except the United States, Canada, and Japan
JIS B4	25.9 × 36.65 cm	Japan
JIS B5	18.36 × 25.9 cm	Japan
U.S. Letter	8.5 × 11 in	United States and Canada
U.S. Legal	8.5 × 14 in	United States and Canada

A very practical study of the many issues to be considered along with many excellent examples can be found in Tony Fernandes's book on global interface design.[26]

NOTES

1. J. E. Beer, "Cross-Cultural Communication Course," Spring 1998, at www.culture-at-work.com/overh1.html#basics (accessed March 1, 2002).

2. Steven John Simon, "A Cross-Cultural Analysis of Web Site Design: An Empirical Study of Global Web Users" at marketing.byu.edu/htmlpages/ccrs/proceedings99/simon.htm (accessed March 1, 2002).

3. G. Hofstede, *Cultures and Organizations: Software of the Mind* (London: McGraw-Hill, 1991).

4. Wendy Clark, "Organisational Culture Theories, Articles, Links," 2001, at www.onepine.demon.co.uk/mcult.htm (accessed March 1, 2002).

5. Aaron Marcus and Emile W. Gould, "Cultural Dimensions and Global Web Design: What? So What? Now What?" 2001, at www.amanda.com/resources/hfweb2000/AM+A.CultDim.pdf (accessed March 1, 2002).

6. Hofstede, *Cultures*, 40.

7. E. W. Gould, N. Zakaria, and S. A. M. Yusof, "Applying Culture to Web Site Design: A Comparison of Malaysian and U.S. Web Sites," *IPCC/SIGDOC 2000. Proceedings Technology Teamwork*: 162 (2000).

8. ITIM Culture and Management Consultants, "National Cultures" at www.itim.org/4aba.html (accessed March 1, 2002).

9. Aaron Marcus and Emile W. Gould at www.amanda.com/resources/hfweb2000/AMA_CultDim.pdf (accessed August 12, 2002).

10. Edward T. Hall, *The Hidden Dimension* (Garden City, N. Y.: Doubleday, 1969); Edward T. Hall, *Beyond Culture* (Garden City, N.Y.: Anchor Press/Doubleday, 1976); Edward T. Hall and Mildred Reed Hall, *Understanding Cultural Differences* (Yarmouth, Maine: Intercultural Press, 1990).

11. Yvonne Cleary, "An Examination of the Impact of Subjective Cultural Issues on the Usability of a Localized Web Site—The Louvre Museum Web Site," 2000, at www.archimuse.com/mw2000/papers/cleary/cleary.html (accessed March 1, 2002).

12. S. W. Chu, "Using Chopsticks and a Fork Together: Challenges and Strategies of Developing a Chinese/English Bilingual Web Site," *Technical Communication Quarterly* 46 (2): 206–19.

13. M. E. Holzschlag "Color My World," 2000, at www.webtechniques. com/archives/2000/09/desi (accessed March 1, 2002).

14. Elke Duncker, Yin Leng Theng, and Norlisa Mohd-Nasir, "Cultural Usability in Digital Libraries," *Bulletin of the American Society for Information Science* 26 (4): 21–22 (April/May 2000).

15. R. Kaplan, "Cultural Thought Patterns in Inter-Cultural Education," *Language Learning* 16: 1–20 (1966).

16. J. M. Ulijn, "Translating the Culture of Technical Documents; Some Experimental Evidence," in *International Dimensions of Technical Communication*, ed. D. C. Andrews (Arlington, Va.: Society for Technical Communication, 1996), 69–89.

17. R. G. Hein, "Culture and Communication," *Technical Communication* 1: 125–27 (1991).

18. B. L. Thatcher, "Cultural and Rhetorical Adaptations for South American Audiences," *Technical Communication* 46 (2): 177–95 (1999).

19. J. Hinds, "Inductive, Deductive, Quasi-Inductive: Expository Writing in Japanese, Korean, Chinese, and Thai," in *Coherence in Writing: Research and Pedagogical Perspective*, ed. U. Connor and A. M. Johns (Alexandria, Va.: Teachers of English to Speakers of Other Languages, 1990), 87–110.

20. S. K. Mayard, "Presentation of One's View in Japanese Newspaper Columns: Commentary Strategies and Sequencing," *Text* 16 (2): 391–421 (1996).

21. T. Kamimura and K. Oi, "A Cross-Cultural Analysis of Argumentative Strategies in Student Essays" (paper presented at the 30th Annual Meeting of the Teachers of English to Speakers of Other Languages, Chicago, Ill., March 1996).

22. W. Fukuoka and J. N. Spyridakis, "The Organization of Japanese Expository Passages," *IEEE Transactions on Professional Communication* 42 (3): 166–74 (1999).

23. Deductive writing places the thesis statement in the initial position with supporting details after the thesis statement. Inductive writing places the thesis statement in the final position with supporting details before the thesis statement.

24. Todd Pierce, *The International Pictograms Standard* (Cincinnati, Ohio: Watson-Guptill Publishers, 1996).

25. Often called the Système International d'Unités or SI.

26. Tony Fernandes, *Global Interface Design* (Boston: AP Professional, 1995), at www.famu.edu/acad/colleges/sbi/dshabazz/global_interface.html/ (accessed March 1, 2002).

REFERENCES

Aykin, N. "Internationalization and Localization of Web Sites." In *8th International Conference on Human Computer Interaction and Special Session on Intelligent Tutoring and Learning Environments,* vol. 1, ed. H. J. Bullinger and J. Ziegler. Mahway, N.J.: Lawrence Erlbaum Associates, 2000.

Betts, Mitch, Carol Sliwa, and Jennifer DiSabatino. "Global Web Sites Prove Challenging," 2000, at www.cnn.com/2000/TECH/computing/08/22/globalization.trials.idg (accessed March 1, 2002).

Cao, L. "Designing for Overseas Chinese Readers: Some Guidelines," 2000, at eserver.org/courses/s01/tc510/adaptivity/cao/cao1.html (accessed March 1, 2002).

Harel, Dan, and Girish Prabhu. "Global User Experience Design (GLUE), Design for Cultural Diversity: Japan, China, and India." In *Designing for Global Markets, Proceedings of First International Workshop on Internationalization of Products and Systems* Rochester, N.Y.: Backhouse Press, 1999.

Hopkins, Robert. "Multilingual Web Sites: A Primer for Webmasters, Authors, and Owners" at www.weblations.com/eng/articles/art_1.htm (accessed March 1, 2002).

Ishida, Richard. "Challenges in Designing International User Information: Cultural Issues," 1998, at www.xerox-emea.com/globaldesign/paper/paper4.htm (accessed March 1, 2002).

Lagon, Olin. "Culturally Correct Site Design" at www.webtechniques.com/archives/2000/09/lagon (accessed March 1, 2002).

Marcus, Aaron. "AM+A Resources" at www.amanda.com/resources/resources_f.html (accessed March 1, 2002).

Marcus, Aaron. "International and Intercultural User Interfaces." In *User Interfaces for All,* ed. Constantine Stephanidis. New York: Lawrence Erlbaum Associates, 2000.

Marcus, Aaron, John Armitage, and Volker Frank. "Globalization of User-Interface Design for the Web," 1999, at zing.ncsl.nist.gov/hfweb/proceedings/marcus (accessed March 1, 2002).

Perlman, Gary. "HCI Bibliography: Intercultural Issues," 2001, at www.hcibib.org/intercultural (accessed March 1, 2002).

Rutherford, Emelie. "How to Avoid Global Web Site Disasters" at www.cio.com/research/global/edit/111400_disaster.html (accessed March 1, 2002).

Rutkowski, Kathy. "Cultural Challenges & the NWEO" at www.gwu.edu/~etlsl20/unit13_culture.htm (accessed March 1, 2002).

Sheridan, E. F., and G. F. Sheridan. "Going Global Online: Monitoring Your Cultural Presence in Cyberspace" at www.webofculture.com/worldsmart/articles/analysis.asp (accessed March 1, 2002).

Training Management Corporation. "Doing Business in China" at www.xerox-emea.com/globaldesign/china.htm (accessed March 1, 2002).

Training Management Corporation. "Doing Business in India" at www.xerox-emea.com/globaldesign/india.htm (accessed March 1, 2002).

Training Management Corporation. "Doing Business in Japan" at www.xerox-emea.com/globaldesign/japan.htm (accessed March 1, 2002).

Training Management Corporation. "Doing Business in Russia" at www.xerox-emea.com/globaldesign/russia.htm (accessed March 1, 2002).

Training Management Corporation. "Doing Business in the U.K." at www.xerox-emea.com/globaldesign/uk.htm (accessed March 1, 2002).

"V for Victory: Five North American Gestures Which Foreigners Might Find Confusing." *Swissair Gazette* (July/August 1997), at www.getcustoms.com/articles/gestures.html (accessed March 1, 2002).

Web of Culture, see especially *WorldSmart* at www.webofculture.com/worldsmart/toc.html (accessed March 1, 2002).

Zahedi, F. M., W. V. Van Pelt, and J. Song. "A Conceptual Framework for International Web Design." *IEEE Transactions on Professional Communication* 44 (2): 83–103.

4

Inputting Content and Translation

GETTING STARTED

The best way to input web content in a variety of languages is to use a multilingual HTML editor, such as Namo WebEditor.[1] Alan Wood provides an additional list of multilingual editors.[2] The editor should have interfaces in a variety of languages, such as Chinese (simplified and traditional), English, German, French, Korean, Japanese, and Spanish. It must either provide the necessary fonts and keyboard drivers or work with Windows keyboards and global input method editors (IMEs). Multilanguage support should also be installed when setting up Windows. If necessary, one should go back and add this feature. To do so in most versions of Windows,[3] select *Start, Settings, Control Panel* and choose *Add/Remove Programs* and then the *Windows Setup* tab. From the list, choose *Multilanguage Support* (see figure 4.1). Click on *Details.* Enable the checkboxes for the languages you want to use, click *OK,* and then click *OK* once more. The support for these languages will install and be available when your computer restarts (see figure 4.2).

Windows Keyboards

Windows allows you to set the keyboard to work with different languages. Access the control panel either through *My Computer/Control Panel/Keyboard* or *Start/Settings/Control Panel/Keyboard.* Depending on the version of the Windows operating system that you are using, select *Language* or *Input Locales/Change* (see figure 4.3). Select *Add* to add a language, followed by *OK* and *Apply.* Make sure

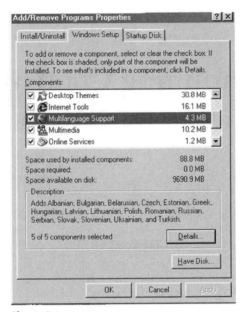

Figure 4.1

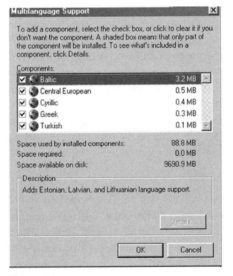

Figure 4.2

Figure 4.3

that *Enable indicator on taskbar* is checked (see figure 4.4). After you have added the languages, examine the bottom or the top of the screen for the language toolbar. *En* will be highlighted (see figure 4.5). By clicking the left mouse button you will be able to switch between the languages that you have added (see figure 4.6).

If you select German, once you start typing, you can press the semicolon (;), apostrophe ('), and left bracket ([) keys to get the *ö*, *ä*, and *ü* symbols, or press Shift+3 to get the β symbol. If you select a Spanish keyboard, the plus (+) and equal (=) symbols will give you the ¡ and ¿ symbols. The problem with this method is that you need keyboard maps in order to know where to find the symbols. One solution is to use Microsoft's Visual Keyboard, which lets you switch keyboard layouts to correspond to the keyboard language you just set up.[4] The keyboard layout appears in a floating window. It works with Windows 95, 98, ME, NT, 2000, XP. It also works with a variety of Microsoft products, including the Office Suite, and with Namo Webeditor. After Visual Keyboard is installed, select *Start/Programs/Microsoft Office Tools/Microsoft Visual Keyboard* (see figure 4.7). When you switch languages, as discussed above, the keyboard display will automatically change (see figure 4.8).

![Keyboard Properties dialog with Add Language dialog showing Language: Afrikaans, Default language English (United States), Switch languages Ctrl+Shift, Enable indicator on taskbar](Figure 4.4)

Figure 4.4

Figure 4.5

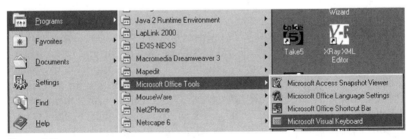

Figure 4.6

![Start menu showing Programs > Microsoft Office Tools > Microsoft Visual Keyboard](Figure 4.7)

Figure 4.7

Figure 4.8

Windows NT

To enable a newly added language and specify a keyboard layout in Windows NT, follow these steps:

Click *Start/Settings/Control Panel.*
Double-click *Regional Settings.*
On the *Regional Settings* tab, click the appropriate language, and then click *Apply.*
Click the *Input Locales* tab.
In the *Input Locales* box, click the appropriate language, and then click *Properties.*
In the *Keyboard Layout* box, click the appropriate keyboard layout, click *OK,* and then click *OK.*

Windows XP

Windows XP has excellent language support. To add languages, do the following:

In the Windows XP standard start menu, click *Start,* and then click *Control Panel.*
In the Windows XP classic start menu, click *Start, Settings,* and then *Control Panel.*
Double-click *Regional and Language Options.*
Click the *Languages* tab, and then click *Details* under *Text Services* and *Input Languages.*
Click *Add* under *Installed Services,* and then click the language you want to add and the keyboard layout you want to use for that language.

To configure the settings for the language bar, click *Language Bar* under *Preferences*.

Input Method Editors

Input method editors, or IMEs, are software tools that allow the website designer to enter text in Asian languages without having to install a Chinese, Japanese, or Korean version of Windows. When an IME is installed, the letters *IME* will appear after the language name in the taskbar at the bottom of the screen (see figure 4.9).[5]

Figure 4.9

TRANSLATION

Considerations

Translation is an important part of any localization project. Content must be available in the language(s) of the target audience(s). Translating internationalized text is easier and faster than translating text that has not been internationalized. Each translator should be fluent in English with a good knowledge of American culture and have a solid grasp of his or her native language and culture. The translation should be complete (not a mixture of English and the native language) and grammatically correct without sounding archaic. The translator must pay attention to the proper use of salutations, local terminology, and the application of formal versus informal verb conjugations used in many languages. For instance, in some Latino cultures everyone is addressed with the formal *usted*. In other Latino cultures it is appropriate to use *usted* (the formal *you*) if the web pages are aimed at adults, and *tu* (the informal *you*) if the web pages are aimed at children. The same is true with *vous* and *tu* in French and *sie* and *du* in German.

Translators must also consider that written French in Canada differs slightly from written French in France. Spanish is written differently in Spain, Central America, Northern South America, and Southern South America. The English term *computer* is *ordenador* in

Spain, *computador* in Mexico and Puerto Rico, and *computadora* in the rest of Latin America. German is written differently in Austria, Switzerland, and Germany. While both the Portuguese and the Brazilians speak Portuguese, there are significant differences in their uses of the language. The importance of a translation that fits with a specific culture is illustrated by the following: If an American says, "I'm mad about my flat," there is something wrong with his car. If an Englishman says it, he likes his apartment. One frequently-cited example is the fact that the word *sale*, which is eye-catching and attractive to an English speaker, means "dirty" in French.[6]

The American Translators Association offers a database of several thousand translators.[7] You can specify language as well as area(s) of expertise. Another good source for translators is Aquarius.[8] Be careful not to forget that JavaScript or other web programs may also need to be translated or localized, as might alt tags and meta tags. If sound or video is being used on the website, these files will also have to be localized.

It is ultimately the responsibility of the website designer to ensure that the translated material has the appropriate text wrapping, punctuation, hyphenation, and spacing.[9] See the discussion in chapter 6 on controlling placement and width of content.

Translation Memory Software

Most translators use one of the many translation memory software programs available on the market.[10] Translation memory software programs create a database that stores translated sentences. They have the following features in common:

- The ability to segment source text by taking the translator automatically to the next source sentence. This feature ensures that no part of the original text is skipped and is typically accomplished using a table or a colored background.
- The ability to remember every sentence, phrase, and word already translated. When a sentence, phrase, or word appears for the second time, the program suggests that the previous translation be used and edited if the context requires.
- The ability to preserve the original typesetting and layout. Translated text will most likely affect the size and layout of page lengths, cell and column sizes in tables, frame sizes, and

line height, as well as the placement of images and line breaks. This, however, is not the concern of the translator, but of the website designer.

Machine Translation

On-the-fly translation tools, often called machine translation or computer-generated translation tools, are adequate for translating a phrase between English and other languages but not for converting a lot of content. Examples of on-the-fly translation tools can be found at AltaVista (babel.altavista.com/translate.dyn) and Systran (www.systransoft.com). Alis Technologies offers—for no charge— Gist-In-Time, which currently can translate up to the equivalent of five printed pages (see figure 4.10).[11] It only translates the HTML part of the page. Graphics and other visual elements will not be translated. The following language pairs are currently covered:

English to French	French to English
English to German	French to German
English to Italian	French to Russian
English to Japanese	German to English
English to Portuguese	German to French
English to simplified Chinese	Italian to English
	Japanese to English
English to Spanish	Portuguese to English
English to traditional Chinese	Spanish to English
	Russian to French

After the program is downloaded and installed, it appears as an option on the *Tools* menu of the Internet Explorer browser (see figure 4.11). The program has also been incorporated into Netscape (since version 6.0) under the *View/Translate* menu (see figure 4.12).

Multilingual Search Engines and Chat Rooms

Website designers may wish to consider adding multilingual search engines and chat rooms. A search on the web will turn up many programs. Atomz Search contains dictionaries and full character-set encodings for Brazilian Portuguese, Czech, Danish, Dutch, European Portuguese, Finnish, French, German, Greek, Italian,

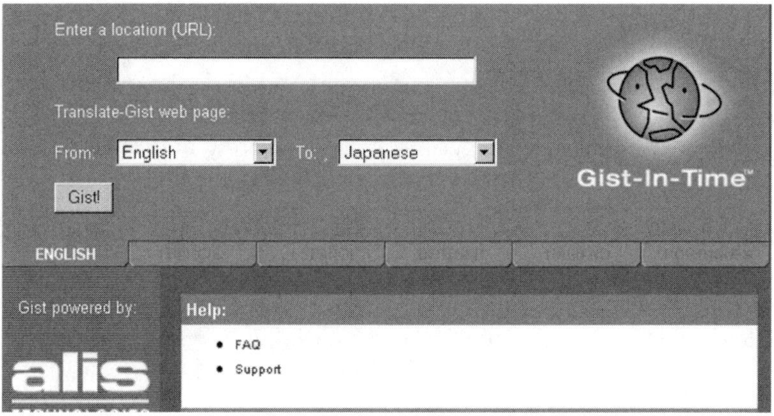

Figure 4.10

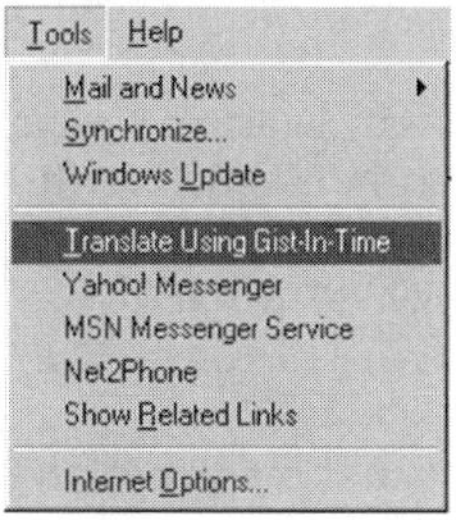

Figure 4.11

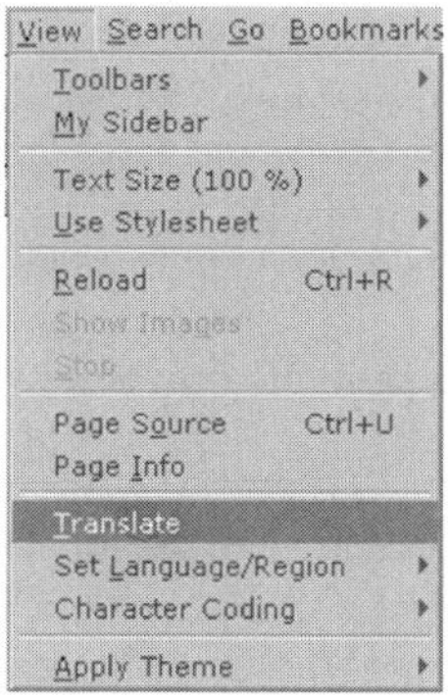

Figure 4.12

Norwegian, Spanish, Slovak, and Swedish. PicoSearch and Mon-
doSearch also work with a variety of languages, including Asian
languages. Inktomi Search works with multiple languages and
character systems, including simplified and traditional Chinese,
Japanese, Korean, Greek, Cyrillic, Arabic, Hebrew, and Thai. Atomz
and PicoSearch offer a free service for smaller websites.[12]

An interesting combination is the merging of Gist-In-Time into the
Copernic Search software.[13] Copernic is a metasearch program that
can sort results from multiple search engines. It can now translate
the results using Gist-In-Time. Multicity.com is an example of a website containing a chat room that can handle 17 different languages.[14]
The chat software is available from the multicity.com website.

NOTES

1. See www.namo.com/products/we4/index.html (accessed March 1,
2002).

2. Alan Wood, "Alan Wood's Unicode Resources: Creating Multilingual
Web Pages: Unicode Support in HTML, HTML Editors and Web Browsers
at www.alanwood.net/unicode/htmlcode.html (accessed March 1, 2002).

3. For instructions on how to add and enable additional languages in
Windows, see http://support.microsoft.com/default.aspx?scid=kb;EN-
US;q177561#Task1.

4. See office.microsoft.com/downloads/2000/viskeyboard.aspx (accessed March 1, 2002).

5. See www.microsoft.com/windows/ie/downloads/recommended/
ime/default.asp (accessed March 1, 2002); "Adding CJK Text with Global
IMEs" at balrog.sdsu.edu/~wstrombe/GlobalIMEweb/Adding_CJK_Text.
htm (accessed March 1, 2002); "Using an IME" at www.andante.org/
ime.html (accessed March 1, 2002); "Using IMEs" at balrog.sdsu.edu/
~wstrombe/Using_the_IME's.htm/ (accessed March 1, 2002).

6. David Travis, "How to Localise Your Website: A UK Perspective on
Usability" at webword.com/moving/global0001.html (accessed March 1,
2002).

7. See www.americantranslators.org/tsd_listings (accessed March 1,
2002).

8. See www.aquarius.net (accessed March 1, 2002).

9. This is especially important with Arabic, Hebrew, and Hindi. If white
space is inserted after vowels used for punctuation, the meaning will be lost.

10. Déjà Vu at www.atril.com (accessed March 1, 2002); Trados 5 at www.
trados.com (accessed March 1, 2002); SDLX at www.sdlintl.com/

products/sdlx/nav/main.htm/ (accessed March 1, 2002); Transit at www.star-ag.ch (accessed March 1, 2002); Wordfast at champollion.net (accessed March 1, 2002); Bert Esselink, "The Difference Between Localization and Translation" at www.languagesnto.org.uk/business/localization.htm (accessed March 1, 2002); Suzanne Assénat-Falcone, "More Translation Memory Tools," *Translation Journal* 4 (2) (April 2000), at accurapid.com/journal/12TM.htm (accessed March 1, 2002).

11. See www.alis.com (accessed March 1, 2002).

12. See atomz.com; www.inktomi.com/products/search/; www.mondosearch.com; www.picosearch.com.

13. See www.copernic.com/downloads (accessed March 1, 2002).

14. Ian Lamont, "Parlez-Vous Multicity?" *Network World,* June 26, 2000, at www.nwfusion.com/news/2000/0626apps.html (accessed March 1, 2002).

REFERENCES

Bradley, Helen. "Speaking in Tongues: Tools Built into Your System and Available on the Web Can Make Your PC Multilingual." *Smart Computing in Plain English* 11 (5): 34–36 (May 2000).

Conroy, Gary. "Technical Writing: Translation and Internationalization" at techwriting.about.com/careers/techwriting/cs/translation/index_2.htm (accessed March 1, 2002).

ETranslate Library at www.etranslate.com/en/index.library.html (accessed March 1, 2002).

European Language and International Strategy. "General Language Resources" at www.elise.dundee.ac.uk/resources_gen.htm (accessed March 1, 2002).

Hopkins, Robert. "Multilingual Web Sites: A Primer for Webmasters, Authors, and Owners" at www.weblations.com/eng/articles/art_1.htm (accessed March 1, 2002).

Ishida, Richard. "Non-Latin Script Characteristics" at www.xerox-emea.com/globaldesign/free.htm#scripts (accessed March 1, 2002).

Lebert, Marie. "Multilingualism on the Web" at www.ceveil.qc.ca/multieng0.htm#home (accessed March 1, 2002).

Lerner, M. "Building Worldwide Web Sites," 1999, at www-106.ibm.com/developerworks/library/web-localization.html (accessed March 1, 2002).

University of Massachusetts, Amherst. "Foreign Language Resource Center" at www.umass.edu/langctr/keyboardhelp.html (accessed March 1, 2002).

5

Using Dynamic XHTML: XHTML and Stylesheets

THE BUILDING BLOCK APPROACH

Recent developments in markup languages and browser capabilities enable the website builder to design a website as a series of building blocks that can be combined in different ways. Broadly speaking, one building block should be content; a second building block should be the interface or the look that you want to give to the content. The content building block is typically coded in HTML, the latest iteration of which is extensible HTML (XHTML). The interface building block is typically coded using CSS.

The building-block technique should be used to build websites for all audiences, but it is especially important when designing for a multinational audience. Typically, you want to deliver the same content to all members of your potential audience. It is the interface or appearance that may need to be adapted for specific audiences. With the building-block approach, you can set up one stylesheet that incorporates features that will make your content appeal to the widest range of users (internationalization), or you can code several different stylesheets based on user preferences or characteristics. Using web programming languages such as JavaScript, VBScript (Visual Basic Script), ASP (Application Server/Pages), ColdFusion, Python, or PHP, you can change the stylesheet and have an entirely different looking site that will appeal to a local audience (localization). Both extensible markup language (XML) and extensible stylesheet language transformations (XSLT) separate content from appearance completely, enabling parts of the same content to be recombined to meet the needs of different communities.

In addition, the files that make up the website should be organized in a sensible fashion. Although the website may be multilingual, each web page is typically monolingual. Some web pages used for navigation might contain multiple languages. Such pages should contain short sections of text, normally no more than one paragraph per language. Otherwise, the web page will become difficult to update.

Language-specific directories should be set up in order to contain all language-specific files. Each directory should be named with its appropriate two-letter language code based on the ISO 639 country and locale specifications (discussed in chapter 2), such as ja for Japanese, fr for French, or es for Spanish (see figure 5.1). In order to differentiate locales, add a two-letter country code, such as fr_CA (Canadian French) and fr_FR (European French) (see figure 5.2). It is also best to use a language preface on all file and graphic names, such as fr_welcome.html, js_welcome.html, or es_welcome.html.

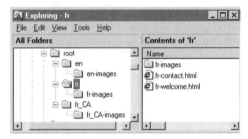

Figure 5.1

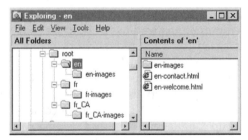

Figure 5.2

HTML, XML, AND XHTML:
UNDERSTANDING THE DIFFERENCES

HTML and XHTML

In 2000, the World Wide Web Consortium (W3C) renamed HTML as XHTML in order to move HTML closer to XML. The current version of XHTML is 1.1. The html tags have not changed, although the word *element* is now preferred to the word *tag*. The real impact is the requirement to write cleaner, more exact code.[1] Appendix 5A at the end of this chapter summarizes the key differences between HTML and XHTML. In addition, the lang attribute (introduced in HTML 4.0) is given new emphasis in XHTML. The lang attribute specifies the language of the content of an element or tag. It can be applied to almost every XHTML element or tag. If you use the lang attribute in an element or tag, you must add the xml:lang attribute. For example:

```
<div xml:lang="fr" lang="fr"> Bonjour Paris!</div>
```

The following is a more complete example:

```
<!DOCTYPE html PUBLIC "-//W3C//DTD XHTML 1.0
Transitional//EN""http://www.w3.org/TR/xhtml1/DTD/
xhtml1-transitional.dtd">
<html xmlns="http://www.w3.org/1999/xhtml"
xml:lang="en-US" lang="en-US" dir = "ltr">
<head>
<meta http-equiv="content-type"
content="text/html; charset=UTF-8" />
<title>Languages test</title>
</head>
<body>
<h1>Languages!</h1>
<p>All of the elements in this document are in
U.S. English except the following:</p>
<p xml:lang="fr" lang = "fr">C&eacute;l&eacute;bre
dans le monde pour son French Cancan,
                            continued on next page
```

```
immortalis&eacute; par Henri de Toulouse-Lautrec,
le Moulin Rouge a toujours pr&eacute;sent&eacute;
aux spectateurs du monde entier de somptueuses
revues: du quadrille de la Goulue et de Valentin-
le-D&eacute;soss&eacute; aux Redoutes et
Op&eacute;rettes, de Colette aux revues &agrave;
grand spectacle de Mistinguett, concept toujours
d'actualit&eacute; sur la sc&egrave;ne du Moulin
Rouge: plumes, strass et paillettes, d&eacute;cors
fabuleux, musiques originales et les plus belles
filles du monde!</p>
<p>This is in English again, since it isn't
contained by the paragraph in English. </p>
</body>
</html>
```

The above example uses special characters to represent the acute and grave accents in French.[2] However, the text could also be written as follows:

```
Célèbre dans le monde pour son French Cancan,
immortalisé par Henri de Toulouse-Lautrec, le
Moulin Rouge a toujours présenté aux spectateurs
du monde entier de somptueuses revues: du
quadrille de la Goulue et de Valentin-le-Désossé
aux Redoutes et Opérettes, de Colette aux revues à
grand spectacle de Mistinguett, concept toujours
d'actualité sur la scène du Moulin Rouge: plumes,
strass et paillettes, décors fabuleux, musiques
originales et les plus belles filles du monde!
```

The Internet Explorer browser will read both versions of the content correctly. The special codes can be used if keyboards are not configured for inputting accents. In addition, the W3C HTML Validation Service (which checks that your web pages are XHTML compliant) cannot reconcile UTF-8 encoding with accents and requires an explicit ISO-8859-1 charset statement in order to validate the second example above as "good" XHTML.[3] Since both English and French will work correctly with the ISO-8859-1 charset, this would not pose a problem for users of this particular web page. However, if other languages were added to the same web page, the encoding should remain as UTF-8. Validators are not perfect and in this case the important thing is not the XHTML validation. The important thing is that the browser correctly displays all the content on the web page.

The Relationship between XHTML and XML

HTML, or XHTML, uses a single, broadly useful set of tags. You use this same set of tags for putting all content onto a web page. The following is a piece of XHTML coding:

```
<table>
<tr>
<td>R. Goldman, J. McHugh, and J. Widom.
<a href="ftp://db.stanford.edu/pub/papers/xml.ps">
From Semistructured Data to XML: Migrating the
Lore Data Model and Query Language
</a>
Proceedings of the 2nd International Workshop on
the Web and Databases
(WebDB '99), pages 25-30, Philadelphia,
Pennsylvania, June 1999.
</td></tr>
<tr><td>
T. Lahiri, S. Abiteboul, and J. Widom.
<a href="ftp://db.stanford.edu/pub/papers/ozone.ps">
Ozone: Integrating Structured and Semistructured
Data
</a>
Technical Report, Stanford Database Group, October
1998.
</td></tr></table>
```

The data has fit into one or more of the generic XHTML tags. As you are limited to one set of tags, it is difficult to focus on the importance of different parts of the data.

The following is the same data coded in XML:[4]

```
<Publication URL="ftp://db.stanford.edu/pub/
papers/xml.ps" Author="RG JM JW">
<Title>From Semistructured Data to XML: Migrating
the Lore Data Model and Query Language</Title>
<Published>Proceedings of the 2nd International
Workshop on the Web and Databases (WebDB
'99)</Published>
<Pages>25-30</Pages>
<Location>
<City>Philadelphia</City>
<State>Pennsylvania</State>
</Location>
<Date>
<Month>June</Month>
<Year>1999</Year>
</Date>
</Publication>
<Publication URL="ft://db.stanford.edu/pub/papers/
ozone.ps" Author="TL SA JW JM">
<Title>Ozone: Integrating Structured and
Semistructured Data</Title>
<Published>Technical Report</Published>
<Institution>Stanford University Database
Group</Institution>
<Date>
<Month>October</Month>
<Year>1998</Year>
</Date>
</Publication>
<Author ID="SA">S. Abiteboul</Author>
<Author ID="RG">R. Goldman</Author>
<Author ID="TL">T. Lahiri</Author>
<Author ID="JM">J. McHugh</Author>
<Author ID="JW">J. Widom</Author>
```

The XML markup accurately describes the content and lets you access the content in a meaningful way, for example by being able to
search for all the papers by author J. Widom, or by all authors with

two or more SIGMOD publications in the same year, or by the earliest publication with "structured data" in its title.

The following is another example that illustrates the importance of meaningful markup tags. Unless you are fluent in Latin, the next few lines might not mean very much:

```
T. Lucreti. Cari.
De Rerum Natura
Liber Primus
Aenaedum genetrix, hominum divomque voluptas
alma Venus, caeli subter labentia signa
quae mare navigerum, quae terras fugiferentis
concelebras, per te quoniam genus omne animantum
concipitur visitque exortum lumina solis.
```

However, if some meaningful markup is added to the jumble of data, then anyone can see what role different parts of the data play in the document.

```
<author>T. Lucreti. Cari. </author>
<title>De Rerum Natura</title>
<chapter>Liber Primus</chapter>
<stanza>Aenaedum genetrix, hominum divomque
voluptas<br />
alma Venus, caeli subter labentia signa <br />
quae mare navigerum, quae terras
frugiferentis<br />
concelebras, per te quoniam genus omne
animantum<br />
concipitur visitque exortum lumina solis.</stanza>
```

A definite document structure is emerging. The markup identifies the author, title, chapter title, and stanza information, including where each line of the stanza ends based on the literary rules to which the poem adheres.

So XML helps identify the meaning of data in a document. If the following page was coded in HTML and you searched for the number $264,000,000, would the number refer to a movie's revenue or budget? With XML markup there is no confusion.

```
<MovieDB>
<Movie Title = "Star Wars: Episode I—The Phantom
Menace" Year = "1999">
<Director>George Lucas</Director>
<Producer>George Lucas</Producer>
<Producer>Rick McCallum</Producer>
<Writer>George Lucas</Writer>
<Actor>Ewan McGregor</Actor>
<Actor>Liam Neeson</Actor>
<Revenue Type="Domestic" USD="427600000"/>
<Revenue Type="International" USD="352100000"/>
</Movie>
<Movie Title="The Sixth Sense" Year="1999"
Runtime= "106">
<Director>M. Night Shyamalan</Director>
<Writer>M. Night Shyamalan</Writer>
<Actor>Bruce Willis</Actor>
<Revenue Type="Domestic" USD="264000000"/>
</Movie>
</MovieDB>
```

We might say that XML is a true use of metadata. The XML tags (designed by you) are metadata—data that add meaning to other data.

Unlike in HTML or XHTML, however, where all you have to think about is the tags, in XML you have to do a lot more work. There are no preset tags. Therefore, the first step when using XML is to create tags (called elements) that will—hopefully—enable users to access different parts of the content in a useful way. The creation of tags or elements is called making a document type definition (DTD). This is itself evolving into schemas. Different industries, groups, and companies are creating collections of markup tags (DTDs). The goal is to develop and standardize data structures as uniformly as possible so that people working in the same field can access data by using the same DTD.

The second step is to code the data using the newly created tags or elements, and the third step is to think about how to present and access the coded data. Unlike HTML, XML has no way to present information.[5] So the final task is to hide the tags or elements by designing an interface using a stylesheet language, such as CSS or exstensible stylesheet language (XSL). Thus, there are many ways to sort and display one set of data. XSL is more powerful than CSS. It provides the ability to display coded XML. It also provides database capabilities for searching and sorting data. XML and XSLT are discussed in more detail in chapter 7.

It is important to understand that XHTML is not XML. XHTML is HTML with some rules added so that HTML and XML and XSL can work together. XHTML will remain the basis for coding content for most general websites. XML, on the other hand, will be used to code descriptive information about collections of related material. In both cases, presentation will be handled by stylesheets, which enable the website designer to tailor interfaces for a multinational audience.

CSS

CSS[6] works with pages coded in HTML, XHTML, and XML and can be used to control the appearance of the website. The stylesheet is stored as a separate file and called into the XHTML pages by the link element or tag. This policy of separating content from appearance makes it easy to, for example, change a font. The new font only has to be recorded once in the stylesheet to take effect in all the XHTML pages. In particular, stylesheets can control fonts (including embedded fonts), tables, the placement and width of elements or tags, the rendering of quotation marks (using : lang pseudo class), the control of bidirectional text (using Unicode-bidi) and the numbering of ordered lists. It is also possible to set the charset via a stylesheet, but it is best to define the charset in the meta tag of each page.

Using Stylesheets to Control Fonts

As mentioned in chapter 2, fonts are required for the visual representation of characters. In the United States, fonts like Arial and Times New Roman are most popular. In general, these fonts can also be used for Western European languages. However, different fonts must be used for Japanese, Korean, traditional Chinese, simplified Chinese, Russian, and other non-Western languages. The following illustrates the use of a style definition to simplify the process of changing fonts:

```
Body{
     font-family: "Times New Roman,"Arial,Verdana;
     font-size:9pt;
}
```

Here is the same style definition after it has been changed for traditional Chinese users. All that is required is a simple change in one location.

```
Body{
     font-family:: MingLiU, PMingLiU;
     font-size:9pt;
}
```

A stylesheet can be used to specify a set of fonts that support a range of languages (see the discussion on fonts in chapter 2).

```
Body{background-color: white; color: black;font-
family: Verdana,Tahoma,"Bitstream
Cyberbit,"Arial;}
```

However, to ensure that the web pages can be read by the intended audiences, it is best to define specific fonts (and alternatives) for specific languages using class selectors. Class selectors can be attached to any XHTML tag or element within the web page. The text should also be marked with the appropriate language attribute. In this way, the website designer is providing as much exact information as possible to the browser as to how the web page should be displayed. The following stylesheet uses class selectors to define fonts and appearance for English, traditional Chinese, Greek, Spanish, Arabic, Russian, Vietnamese, and simplified Chinese text. Note also the definition of line height. East Asian languages require 30 percent greater height per character.

```
.en {font-family: 'Times New Roman'; color:black;}

.cht {font-family: MingLiU,PMingLiU,'Bitstream
Cyberbit','Bitstream CyberCJK','UWCXMF (Big5)';
line-height: 150%; background-color: white; color:
blue; }

.gr { font-family: 'Times New Roman';background-
color:white; color:pink; }

.es { font-family: 'Times New Roman'; background-
color:white; color:green }

.ar{font-family: 'Transparent Arabic'; background-
color:white; color:blue;}
.ru {font-family: 'Times New Roman'; background-
color:white; color:red;}
.vi {font-family: 'Times New Roman'; background-
color:white; color:orange;}
.chs {font-family: "MS Hei"; background-
color:white; color:black; }
```

The XHTML page could be coded as follows. The stylesheet is stored as a separate file (example.css) and is called into the XHTML pages by means of the link element or tag.

```
<!DOCTYPE html PUBLIC "-//W3C//DTD XHTML 1.0
Transitional//EN""http://www.w3.org/TR/xhtml1/DTD/
xhtml1-transitional.dtd">
<html xmlns="http://www.w3.org/1999/xhtml"
xml:lang="en-US" lang="en-US" dir="ltr">
<head>
<meta http-equiv="content-type"
content="text/html; charset=UTF-8" />
<title>Example Page</title>
<meta http-equiv="keywords" content="list of
keywords for searching" />
```
continued on next page

```
<meta name="Author" content="Linda Main" />
<link rel="stylesheet" type="text/css"
href="example.css" />
</head>
<body>
<h1>English Title</h1>
<p xml:lang = "en" lang = "en" class = "en" dir =
"ltr">English text
<br /><a href=" English.html"> English
description</a>
</p>
<p xml:lang="zh-tw" lang =zh-tw" class = "cht">
Traditional Chinese </p>
<p xml:lang="gr" lang = "gr" class = "gr">
Greek</p>
<p xml:lang="es" lang = "es" class = "es">
Spanish</p>
<h1 xml:lang="ar" lang="ar" dir="rtl" class="ar" >
<bdo>Arabic description</bdo>
</h1>
<br />
<p xml:lang="ar" lang = "ar" dir = "rtl" class =
"ar" ><bdo>Arabic description</bdo></p>
<p xml:lang="ri" lang = "ru" class = "ru">
Russian</p>
<p xml:lang="vi" lang = "vi" class =
"vi">Vietnamese</p>
<p xml:lang="zh-cn" lang="zh-cn" class="chs">Lots
of simplified Chinese text </p>
</body>
</html>
```

Figure 5.3 shows the result in Internet Explorer.

Embedded Fonts

CSS offers the ability to download a specific embedded font[7] using the @font-face instruction (part of the At-Rule options of CSS). This technique can be used to make available fonts for less-common languages. All @font-face instructions should go at the beginning of

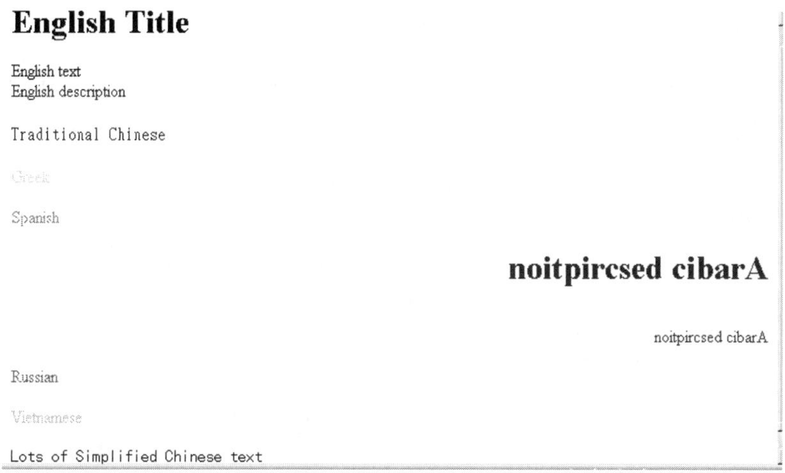

English Title

English text
English description

Traditional Chinese

Greek

Spanish

noitpircsed cibarA

noitpircsed cibarA

Russian

Vietnamese

Lots of Simplified Chinese text

Figure 5.3

the stylesheet. The instruction consists of at least a font name to reference the font and the URL of the OpenType file. Font styles can also be set as the following stylesheet code example demonstrates:

```
@font-face {font-family: Mangal; font-style:
normal; font-weight: normal;      src:
url(http://senna.sjsu.edu/lmain/eot/MANGAL0.eot); }
@font-face {font-family: Latha; font-style:
normal; font-weight: normal; src:
url(http://senna.sjsu.edu/lmain/eot/LATHA0.eot); }
.hindi {font-family: Mangal;  background-
color:white; color:black; }
.tamil {font-family: Latha; background-
color:white;    color:black; }
```

The .hindi and .tamil class selectors can then be used in the appropriate place in the XHTML coding. For example:

```
<p class = "hindi">This text is in Mangal font </p>
```

Using Stylesheets to Control Tables

Tables are an important building block for web pages. The following example uses a table to control layout. The table is defined in the stylesheet, as are explicit fonts for various languages using class selectors. The span element or tag is defined so that when an English word or phrase occurs in non-Latin text, it is possible to specify a font just for that word or phrase.

```
table {width: 700; font-family : Arial; font-size :
10pt; font-weight: normal; font-style: normal;
border-width: 10px; border-color:red; border-
style: solid; align:center}
tr { width: 680; text-align:center; font-family :
Arial; font-size: 10pt; font-weight: normal; font-
style : normal; }
td { width: 580; text-align:center; font-family:
Arial; font-size : 10pt; font-weight: normal;
font-style: normal; background-color: #cc99ff;}
span {font-family: Verdana,Tahoma,Bitstream
CyberBase,Arial; }
.en {font-family: 'Times New Roman'; color:black; }
.cht {font-family: MingLiU,PMingLiU,'Bitstream
Cyberbit','Bitstream CyberCJK','UWCXMF (Big5)';
line-height: 150%; background-color: red; color:
blue; }
.gr { font-family: 'Times New Roman'; background-
color:white; color:pink; }
.es {font-family: 'Times New Roman'; background-
color:white; color:green}
.ar{font-family: 'Transparent Arabic'; background-
color:white; color:blue;}
.ru {font-family: 'Times New Roman'; background-
color:white; color:red; }
.vi {font-family: 'Times New Roman'; background-
color:white; color:orange; }
.chs font-family: "MS Hei"; background-
color:white; color:black; }
...and so on for various languages...
```

The following is a partial example of the coding. The text is marked with the language attribute. This helps to ensure that the browser selects the correct fonts.

```
<!DOCTYPE html PUBLIC "-//W3C//DTD XHTML 1.0
Transitional//EN""http://www.w3.org/TR/xhtml1/DTD/
xhtml1-transitional.dtd">
<html xmlns="http://www.w3.org/1999/xhtml"
xml:lang="en-US" lang="en-US" dir="ltr">
<head>
<meta http-equiv="content-type"
content="text/html; charset=UTF-8" />
<title>Example Page</title>
<meta http-equiv="keywords" content="list of
keywords for searching" />
<meta name="Author" content="Linda Main" />
<link rel="stylesheet" type="text/css"
href="exampletable.css" />
</head>
<body>
<table>
<tbody>
<tr>
<td xml:lang = "en" lang="en"><b>Arabic
</b></td></tr>
<tr>
<td xml:lang = "ar" lang="ar" dir="rtl" class =
"ar"><bdo>Arabic Text</bdo></td></tr>
<tr>
<td xml:lang = "en" lang="en"><b>Chinese
(simplified)</b></td></tr>
<tr>
<td xml:lang = "zh-cn" lang="zh-cn" class =
"chs">simplified Chinese text</td></tr>
<tr>
<td xml:lang = "en" lang="en"><b>Irish Gaelic
</b></td></tr
<tr>
```
continued on next page

```
<td xml:lang = "ga" lang="ga">Irish Gaelic
text</td></tr>
...and so on for all languages....
</tbody>
</table>
</body>
</html>
```

Figures 5.4 to 5.8 show the resulting output. The translations are used for purposes of illustration and are taken from the translations set up for the Tenth International Unicode Conference.[8]

Arabic

أوروبا, برمجيات الحاسوب + انترنيت :
تصبح عالميا مع يونيكود

تسجّل الآن لحضور المؤتمر الدولي العاشر ليونيكود, الذي سيعقد في 10-12 آذار 1997 بمدينة ماينتس, ألمانيا. وسيجمع المؤتمر بين خبراء من كافة قطاعات الصناعة على الشبكة العالمية انترنيت ويونيكود, حيث ستتم, على الصعيدين الدولي والمحلي على حد سواء مناقشة سبل استخدام يونكود في النظم القائمة وفيما يخص التطبيقات الحاسوبية, الخطوط, تصميم النصوص والحوسبة متعددة اللغات.

عندما يريد العالم أن يتكلّم, فهو يتحدّث بلغة يونيكود.

Figure 5.4

Chinese (Simplified)

欧洲，软件＋互联网
用统一码 (Unicode) 走遍世界

将于1997年 3 月10日－12日在德国 Mainz 市举行的第十届统一码国际研讨会现在开始注册。本次会议将汇集各方面的专家。涉及的领域包括：国际互联网和统一码，国际化和本地化，统一码在操作系统和应用软件中的实现，字型，文本格式以及多文种计算等。

当世界需要沟通时，请用Unicode！

Figure 5.5

歐洲，軟體及網際網路：
讓統一碼（Unicode）領你進入全世界

你現在就應報名將在１９９７年３月１０至１２日於德國美姿城（Mainz）召開的第十屆國際統一碼研討會。本次研討會將邀請多位業界專家研討關於全球網際網路及統一碼發展、國際化及本土化、支援統一碼的作業系統及應用程式、字型、文字排版、電腦多國語文化等多項課題。

當世界需要溝通時，請用統一碼（Unicode）

Figure 5.5 *Continued*

אירופה, תוכנה והאינטרנט:
יוצא לשוק העולמי Unicode

הירשמו כעת לכנס Unicode הבינלאומי העשירי, שייערך בין התאריכים 12‑10 במרץ 1997, במיינץ שבגרמניה. בכנס ישתחפו מומחים מכל ענפי החעשייה בנשא האינטרנט העולמי וה‑Unicode, בהתאמה לשוק הבינלאומי והמקומי, ביישום Unicode במערכות הפעלה ובייושומים, בגופנים, בפריסת טקסט ובמחשוב רב‑לשוני.

כאשר העולם רוצה לדבר, הוא מדבר ב‑Unicode

Európa, a Szoftver s az Internet -
Globálissá Változik a Unicode Által

Iratkozzon már most a Tizedik Nemzetközi Unicode Konferenciára, amely Március 10-12 1997 lesz megtartva, Meinz-be, Németországba. Ebben a Konferencián az iparág szerte sok szakértő fog részt venni: a globális Internet s Unicode nemzetközisítése s lokalizálása, a Unicode beteljesítése a működő rendszerekben s alkalmazásokban, fontokba, szöveg térbeosztásba s többnyelvű computerekben.

Figure 5.6

ヨーロッパ、ソフトウェア、そしてインターネット：
Unicode でグローバル化を狙って

第 10 回の Unicode 会議は 1997 年 3 月 10～12日、ドイツのマインツで開かれます。参加希望の方は今すぐ登録してください。この会議では、グローバルなインターネット、Unicode、ソフトウェアの国際化およびローカリゼーション、OS およびアプリケーションでの Unicode のインプリメンテーション、フォント、テキスト表示、マルチ言語コンピューティングにおける業界の専門家が集まります。

世界的に話すなら、Unicode です。

Figure 5.7

Korean

유럽, 소프트웨어 그리고 인터넷:
유니코드와 함께 세계로

제10회 유니코드 국제 회의가 1997년 3월 10일부터 12일까지 독일의 마인즈에서
열립니다. 지금 등록하십시오. 이 회의에서는 업계 전반의 전문가들이 함께 모여
다음과 같은 분야를 다룹니다. - 인터넷과 유니코드, 국제화와 지역화, 운영 체제와
응용 프로그램에서 유니코드의 구현, 글꼴, 문자 배열, 다국어 컴퓨팅.
세계를 향한 대화, 유니코드로 하십시오

Figure 5.7   Continued

Russian

Европа, Программное обеспечение + Интернет:
Unicode в глобальных масштабах

Зарегистрируйтесь сейчас на Десятую Международную Конференцию по Unicode,
которая состоится 10-12 марта 1997 года в Майнце в Германии. Конференция соберет
широкий круг экспертов по вопросам глобального Интернета и Unicode, локализации и
интернационализации, воплощению и применению Unicode в различных
операционных системах и программных приложениях, шрифтах, верстке и
многоязычных компьютерных системах.
Когда мир желает общаться, он общается на Unicode

Slovenian

Evropa, programje in Internet:
globalizacija z Unicodom

Prijavite se na Deseto mednarodno konferenco Unicode, ki bo med 10. in 12. marcem v Mainzu,
Nemčija. Konferenca bo zbrala svetovno znane izvedence za globalni Internet in Unicode,
internacionalizacijo in lokalizacijo, izvedbe Unicode v različnih operacijskih sistemih in programe,
fonte, stavljenje besedila in večjezično računalništvo.
Ko se želi svet pogovarjati, govori Unicode

Figure 5.8

Using Absolute Positioning to Control Placement and Width

If you want to use the same layout for content in a variety of languages, it is important to remember that text translated from English
into other European languages typically grows by 30 to 40 percent.
For example, the word *news* is generally *actualités* in French, which
requires more than twice the space of the English word. A word
translated from English to Hindi might increase by 80 percent. However, English words translated into some Asian languages shrink. As
a result, it is best to use absolute positioning to control placement

and width of, for example, table columns, table cells, drop down lists, frame sizes, line breaks, line heights, and so on (making sure that enough space is left for the widest translated text). However, first let's consider static, relative, absolute, and fixed positioning.

Static positioning deals with how a web browser lays out pages. A Web browser takes an XHTML file, parses it into its elements or tags, applies styles from a stylesheet, and then flows the elements onto the page. The position that a tag or element, such as a paragraph, has in this flow is its static position.

Relative positioning places an element with respect to where it would statically be positioned. When you relatively position an element, you are saying to a browser, "Take this paragraph and put it 10 px down and 10 px to the right of where it would normally be." With a relative position, a top of 20 px and a left of 20 px places a tag or element 20 px to the right and 20 px down from where it would naturally, or statically, be located.

Absolute positioning lets a designer say where the top left-hand corner of an element or tag should be located with respect to its parent element.[9] Both start and end points and all dimensions (top, left, width, etc.) can be specified and easily changed. If, for example, you have web pages in a variety of languages, you may decide to list the available languages in a drop down list on your opening page. The Hewlett Packard website uses a drop down list, but the complete contents of the list are in the language selected by the user.[10] It is better to have a drop down list of all available languages on all pages so that a language switch option is available throughout the website. This solution works better than using flags. To represent German do you use the German flag or the Swiss or Austrian flag? Some Namibians speak German. The Spanish flag could represent the Spanish language as spoken in Spain, but what about all the other countries that speak Spanish, such as Peru or Colombia? Of course, using a drop down list does not solve the problem of the order of languages or countries in a list.

The following stylesheet code will position the list in the top right-hand corner of the web page (see figure 5.9). The list will remain there no matter what other code is added to the page. It may be that you position the list on the left-hand side of the page. Much will depend on the reading culture of the target audience. In Westernized cultures, the most important objects on a web page should appear in the upper left corner; important objects should be positioned in the upper right corner for users in Israel or in East Asian and Arabic countries. In either case, the list can be locked into position.

```
select {position:absolute; top: 0.5px; right:0;
font-size:120%;width:170px;margin:8px,3px;}
```

The XHTML coding could be as follows:

```
<!DOCTYPE html PUBLIC "-//W3C//DTD XHTML 1.0
Transitional//EN""http://www.w3.org/TR/xhtml1/DTD/
xhtml1-transitional.dtd">
<html xmlns="http://www.w3.org/1999/xhtml"
xml:lang="en-US" lang="en-US" dir="ltr">
<head>
<meta http-equiv ="content-type"
content="text/html; charset=UTF-8" />
<link rel="stylesheet" type="text/css"
href="langlinks.css" />
<title></title>
</head>
<body bgcolor="ffffff">
<select name="langlinks" id = "langlinks" size =
"10">
<option value="ru">&#1056;&#1091;&#1089;&#1089;
&#1082;&#1080;&#1081;
<option value="hk">&#20013;&#25991; (HK)
</option>
<option value="cn">&#20013;&#25991; (CN)
</option>
<option value="fr">Fran&ccedil;ais</option>
<option value = "en">English</option>
<option value = "pt">Portugu&ecirc;s </option>
<option value = "ro">Rom&acirc;n&#259;</option>
<option value = "tu">T&uuml;rk&ccedil;e</option>
<option value = "gr">&#917;&#955;&#955;&#951;
&#957;&#953;&#954;&#940; (Ellynika)</option>
<option value = "es">Espa&ntilde;ol</option>
</select>
</body>
</html>
```

If you add the attribute size = "10" to the select tag, the complete list will remain visible. A user can read and select the name of his or her language in that language (see figure 5.10). In the next chapter we will add some hidden JavaScript so that when a selection is made, the user will automatically be taken to web pages in the language of choice.

Figure 5.9

Figure 5.10

Fixed positioning permits the web designer to position tags or elements with respect to the top of the window. In the following stylesheet, note that the position of the table is fixed on the page. Note also that the select list is positioned absolutely in regard to its position, width, and height (see figure 5.11).

```
table
{position:fixed; top: 100px; left: 100px; bottom:
30px; right: 40px;background-color: #f0aa28;
border-collapse: collapse; border-spacing: 0px;
border: 2px black solid; width: 80%; margin-left:
10%; margin-right: 10%;}
td {background-color: #e3911d; border: 2px black
solid; padding: 1%; width: 25%; }
                            continued on next page
```

```
.titlebar {background-color: #000000; color:
white; font-size: 2em; font-weight: bold; padding:
.15em; text-align: center}
.label {background-color: #e4be6d; font-weight: bold}
.picture {background-color: #e4be6d; text-align:
center}
.news {height: 170px}
select {position:absolute; top: 170px; left: 90
px; width:120px; height:170px;}
```

The XHTML coding (with the menu list open) would look as follows:

```
<!DOCTYPE html PUBLIC "-//W3C//DTD XHTML 1.0
Transitional//EN""http://www.w3.org/TR/xhtml1/DTD/
xhtml1-transitional.dtd">
<html xmlns="http://www.w3.org/1999/xhtml"
lang="en-US" xml:lang="en-US" dir="ltr">
<head>
<title>Tables</title>
<meta http-equiv="content-type"
content="text/html; charset=UTF-8" />
<meta http-equiv= "keywords" content="list of
keywords for searching" />
<meta name="Author; content="Linda Main" />
<link rel="stylesheet" type="text/css"
href="table.css" />
</head>
<body>
<table>
<tr>
<td colspan="4" class="titlebar">Senna</td>
</tr>
<tr>
<td rowspan="2" class="picture"><img
src="senna.jpg" alt="Senna" width = "90" height =
"90" alt = "pictures of senna"/></td>
<td class="label">Origin</td>
<td class="label">Biological Name</td>
<td class="label">Available?</td>
```
                                    continued on next page

```
</tr>
<tr>
<td>N. Africa,India, Pakistan,China</td>
<td>LeguminosaeCassia acutiplia</td>
<td><a href="http://slisweb.sjsu.edu">Buy Now</a>
</td>
</tr>
<tr>
<td class="news"><select name = "langlinks" id =
"langlinks" size = "10">
<option value="ru">&#1056;&#1091;&#1089;&#1089;
&#1082;&#1080;&#1081; </option>
<option value="hk">&#20013;&#25991; (HK)
</option>
<option value="cn">&#20013;&#25991; (CN)
</option>
<option value="fr">Fran&ccedil;ais</option>
<option value = "en">English</option>
<option value = "pt">Portugu&ecirc;s </option>
<option value = "ro">Rom&acirc;n&#259;</option>
<option value = "tu">T&uuml;rk&ccedil;e</option>
<option value = "gr">&#917;&#955;&#955;&#951;
&#957;&#953;&#954;&#940; (Ellynika)</option>
<option value = "es">Espa&ntilde;ol</option>
</select></td>
<td colspan="3"> Cassia senna is native to
tropical Africa and cultivated in Egypt and the
Sudan. Cassia angustifolia is native to India and
cultivated mainly in India and Pakistan. In some
parts of the world, the leaves are made into a
paste and applied to various skin diseases.</td>
</tr>
<tr>
<td class="label">Medicinal Uses</td>
<td colspan="3">Senna is a powerful cathartic used
in the treatment of constipation. It works through
a stimulation of intestinal peristalsis.</td>
</tr>
</table>
</body>
</html>
```

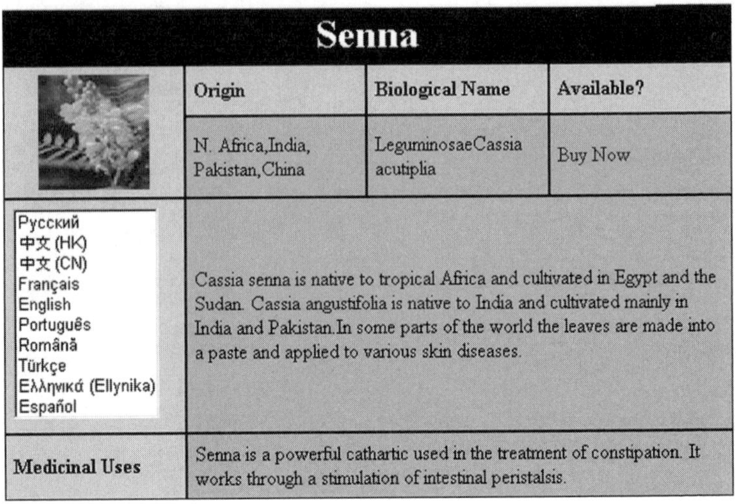

Senna			
	Origin	**Biological Name**	**Available?**
	N. Africa,India, Pakistan,China	LeguminosaeCassia acutiplia	Buy Now
Русский 中文 (HK) 中文 (CN) Français English Português Română Türkçe Ελληνικά (Ellynika) Español	Cassia senna is native to tropical Africa and cultivated in Egypt and the Sudan. Cassia angustifolia is native to India and cultivated mainly in India and Pakistan.In some parts of the world the leaves are made into a paste and applied to various skin diseases.		
Medicinal Uses	Senna is a powerful cathartic used in the treatment of constipation. It works through a stimulation of intestinal peristalsis.		

Figure 5.11

Using the @import Rule

It might be useful to set up a generic stylesheet defining features common to all web pages in all languages. Each individual language could have its own language-specific stylesheet and the generic stylesheet can be called into each one using the @import rule. The @import statement should come at the top of the stylesheet. For example:

```
@import "common.css";
body {font-family: MingLiU,PMingLiU,'Bitstream
Cyberbit','Bitstream CyberCJK','UWCXMF (Big5)';
line-height: 150%; background-color: white; color:
blue; }
```

Using :lang Pseudo Class to Display Quotes

The :lang pseudo class in CSS is a way to further enhance various tags or elements. Different languages have different formatting conventions for quotation marks, italics, bold, indenting, and so on. Listed below are just a few examples showing how each language handles nested quotes (quotes within quotes):

```
»Dansk 'da' Danish«
„Deutsch 'de' German"
"English 'en' English"
« Français « fr » French »
«Italiano «it» Italian»
«Norsk 'no' Norwegian»
« CAA:89 „ru" Russian»
```

In CSS, the actual quotation marks that will be drawn are defined by the quotes property. Quotes are thought of as a list of pairs of strings. Each pair defines respectively the opening and the closing quotation mark. The pairs are separated by spaces, as is each element of a pair. This property allows different quotation marks to be created for different elements or tags. The following example uses the q element or tag.

```
q:lang(en) {quotes: '"' '"' "'" "'" }
q:lang(fr) {quotes: "«" "»" "<" ">" }
```

In English, according to this statement, first level quotes are double quoted, while second level quotes are single quoted. In French, first level quotes use "«" and "»" while second level quotes use "<" and ">."

In the next example, the rule sets the type of quotation marks for an XHTML document that is in Norwegian.

```
ql:lang(no) { quotes: '« ' ' »' "" "" }
```

In the final example, the rule sets the type of quotation marks for block quote elements or tags. This example does not define nested quotes.

```
blockquote:lang(no){ quotes: '« ' ' »' }
```

Using Unicode-bidi to Control Direction

The Unicode-bidi property is used when you need to display bidirectional text. Bidirectional text is written right-to-left with left-to-right text interspersed to handle foreign words or numbers. Unicode-bidi works with the direction property that sets the direction in which the text flows. For example:

```
html {direction:rtl;}
blockquote {direction:ltr}
div { direction: rtl; unicode-bidi:bidi-override}
td {direction: rtl; unicode-bidi: bidi-override}
.rtl {
direction: rtl; unicode-bidi: embed; display:
block; font-size: 1.2em;
}
.ltr { direction: ltr; unicode-bidi: embed;
display: block; font-size: 1.2em;
}
.reverse {direction: rtl; unicode-bidi:bidi-
override; display: inline;
text-decoration: underline;
}
.appearance {display: inline; font-weight: bold; }
```

In this stylesheet, the direction is set in the html tag as right-to-left (see figure 5.12). However, note that this causes characters to start on the right and move left. As discussed in chapter 2, merely setting the direction right-to-left of itself does not affect the direction of the actual letters because directionality is implicit to the text. The letters are implicitly left-to-right as can be seen in the rendering of the text between the <p></p> tags. This can be changed when Unicode-bidi is set to bidi-override, which overrides the default behavior as in the div and td style definitions above. The two class selectors of .rtl and .ltr use Unicode-embed. The text that is mostly Hebrew is the part controlled by the .rtl selector; that which is mostly English is the part controlled by the .ltr selector. The .reverse selector permits the use of right-to-left words within the left-to-right defined paragraph. The XHTML coding follows:

```
<!DOCTYPE html PUBLIC "-//W3C//DTD XHTML 1.0
Transitional//EN""http://www.w3.org/TR/xhtml1/DTD/
xhtml1-transitional.dtd">
<html xmlns="http://www.w3.org/1999/xhtml"
xml:lang="en-US" lang="en-US">
<head>
<meta http-equiv="content-type"
content="text/html;charset=UTF-8"/>
<title></title>
<link rel="stylesheet" type="text/css"
href="bid1.css" />
<body bgcolor="ffffff"><font size = "4">
<blockquote>
ABC DEF GHI JKL MNO PQR STV UWX YZ.
</blockquote>
<p>Linda Main is a teacher at San Jose State
University.</p>
<div>Linda Main is a teacher at San Jose State
University.</div>
<table border = "5"><tr><td>Linda Main</td><td>San
Jose State</td></tr></table>
<p class = "rtl">&#x5D0;&#x5D1;&#x5D2;1
&#x5D0;&#x5D1;&#x5D2;2 abc3 &#x5D0;&#x5D1;&#x5D2;4
&#x5D0;&#x5D1;&#x5D2;5</p>
<p class = "rtl">&#x5D0;&#x5D1;&#x5D2;6 <span
class = "appearance">&#x5D0;&#x5D1;&#x5D2;7</span>
&#x5D0;&#x5D1;&#x5D2;8</p>
<Ltr>
<p class = "ltr">abc9 abc10 abc11
&#x5D0;&#x5D1;&#x5D2;12
&#x5D0;&#x5D1;&#x5D2;13</p>
<p class = "ltr">abc14 abc15
&#x5D0;&#x5D1;&#x5D2;16</p>
<p class = "ltr">abc17<span class =
"reverse">Linda&#x5D0;&#x5D1;&#x5D2;18 abc19 abc20
&#x5D0;&#x5D1;&#x5D2;21</span> abc22
&#x5D0;&#x5D1;&#x5D2;23</p>
</Ltr>
</body>
</html>
```

ABC DEF GHI JKL MNO PQR STV UWX YZ.

.Linda Main is a teacher at San Jose State University

.ytisrevinU etatS esoJ naS ta rehcaet a si niaM adniL

| etatS esoJ naS | niaM adniL |

5אגב 4אגב abc3 2אגב 1אגב

8אגב 7**אבג** 6אגב

abc9 abc10 abc11 13אגב 12אגב

abc14 abc15 16אגב

abc1712אגב 02cba 91cba 81אגבadniL abc22 23אגב

Figure 5.12

Numbering Ordered Lists

There are many different numbering systems for ordering list items:

- Decimal (decimal numbers, beginning with 1);
- Decimal-leading-zero (decimal numbers padded by initial zeros [e.g., 01, 02, 03, . . . , 99]);
- Lower-roman (lowercase roman numerals [i, ii, iii, iv, v, . . .]);
- Upper-roman (uppercase roman numerals [I, II, III, IV, V, . . .]);
- Lower-Latin or lower-alpha (lowercase ASCII letters [a, b, c, . . .]);
- Upper-Latin or upper-alpha (uppercase ASCII letters [A, B, C, . . .]);
- Lower-Greek (lowercase classical Greek alpha, beta, gamma, . . . [έ, ή, ί, . . .];
- Hebrew (traditional Hebrew numbering);
- Georgian (traditional Georgian numbering [an, ban, gan, . . . , he, tan, in, in-an, . . .]);
- Armenian (traditional Armenian numbering);
- CJK-ideographic (plain ideographic numbers);
- Hiragana (a, i, u, e, o, ka, ki, . . .);
- Katakana (A, I, U, E, O, KA, KI, . . .);
- Hiragana-iroha (i, ro, ha, ni, ho, he, to, . . .);
- Katakana-iroha (I, RO, HA, NI, HO, HE, TO, . . .);

A stylesheet definition (using class selectors) might read as follows:

```
.decimal { list-style-type: decimal}
.lroman {list-style-type: lower-roman}
.uroman {list-style-type: upper-roman}
.hiragana {list-style-type: hiragana-iroha}
.greek {list-style-type: lower-greek}
```

The web page coding would read as follows:

```
<ol class="decimal">
<li>Dogs</li>
<li>Cats</li>
<li>Fish</li>
</ol>
<ol class="lroman">
<li>Dogs</li>
<li>Cats</li>
<li>Fish</li>
</ol>
<ol class="uroman">
<li>Dogs</li>
<li>Cats</li>
<li>Fish</li>
</ol>
<ol class="hiragana">
<li>Dogs</li>
<li>Cats</li>
<li>Fish</li>
</ol>
<ol class="greek">
<li>Dogs</li>
<li>Cats</li>
<li>Fish</li>
</ol>
```

Setting Encoding Using a Stylesheet

It is possible to set the encoding for the web page in an external stylesheet by using the @charset At-Rule. The @charset At-Rule is allowed to occur only once in an external stylesheet, and it must be the very first statement in the stylesheet. It supersedes any encoding declarations specified in the document that reference the stylesheet. For example:

```
@charset "UTF-8";
```

This should not be used if the stylesheet commands are embedded into a web page (as opposed to being called from the external stylesheet). As mentioned above however, it is best to have the charset explicitly stated in each web page.

CSS3

CSS3, which is under development, will provide better control over line and word breaking and direction. The writing property will replace direction; ltr and rtl will be replaced by lr-tb (left-to-right and top-to-bottom), rl-tb (right-to-left and top-to-bottom), tb-rl (top-to-bottom and right-to-left), and so on. CSS3 will also provide better support for ruby text, which is text that sits close to another run of text. It is used to indicate pronunciation in Chinese and Japanese.[11]

NOTES

1. The HomeSite Editor (running Tidy) converts HTML pages into XHTML (http://www.macromedia.com/software/homesite).
2. Webmonkey, "Special Characters and Entities" at hotwired.lycos.com/webmonkey/reference/special_characters (accessed March 1, 2002).
3. See validator.w3.org.
4. Like HTML, XML is actually a subset of standard generalized markup language, or SGML.
5. It is possible to code presentation directly in HTML using tags for font, bold, etc. This approach is no longer recommended, and presentation should be coded in CSS as discussed in the text. However, it is still techni-

cally possible to use tags for font and bold. It is not technically possible in XML, which completely separates content from presentation.

6. CSS1 came into use in 1996. In 1998, CSS2 added support for downloadable fonts, element positioning, and tables.

7. Embedded fonts are discussed in chapter 2.

8. "Tenth International Unicode Conference: Language," 1997, at www.unicode.org/iuc/iuc10/x-utf8.html (accessed March 1, 2002; "Tenth International Unicode Conference: Credits," 1997, at www.unicode.org/iuc/iuc10/credits.html (accessed March 1, 2002).

9. Note that it is not with respect to the top left-hand corner of the page.

10. See www.itrc.hp.com.

11. Michael Suignard, "CSS3 Text Extensions," in *18th International Unicode Conference*, Hong Kong, 2001, at www.microsoft.com/globaldev/Presentations/18th_Unicode_Conf.asp (accessed March 1, 2002), for notes in Word or Adobe format.

REFERENCES

Cunningham, Andrew. "Multilingual Unicode Web Page Development." In *Community Networking Conference 1999: Engaging Regionalism.* edited by A. Funston. Victoria, Australia: Ballarat University, 1999, at members.ozemail.com.au/~andjc/papers/cn99.html (accessed March 1, 2002).

Ishida, Richard. "Helping Users Navigate to the Right Localised Site." In *18th International Unicode Conference.* Hong Kong, 2001, at www.xerox-emea.com/globaldesign/free.htm#navigation (accessed March 1, 2002).

Korpela, Jukka. "HTML Authoring in Different Languages" at www.malibutelecom.fi/yucca/html/languages.html (accessed March 1, 2002).

Maribyrnong Library Service at library.maribyrnong.vic.gov.au/ (accessed March 1, 2002).

Nelson, Paul. "Authoring HTML for Middle Eastern Content" at www.microsoft.com/globaldev/articles/mideast.asp (accessed March 1, 2002).

Port Phillip Library Service. "PPLS Sling: A Web of Languages" at home.vicnet.net.au/~ppls/sling/lotemain.htm (accessed March 1, 2002).

W3C. "World-Wide Character Sets, Languages, and Writing Systems" at www.w3.org/International (accessed March 1, 2002).

APPENDIX 5A: DIFFERENCES
BETWEEN HTML AND XHTML

DOCTYPE

An XHTML web page consists of four main parts delineated by the <DOCTYPE>, <html>, <head>, and <body> tags. The difference from the template typically used in HTML web pages is the addition of the DOCTYPE.

```
<!DOCTYPE ...>
<html>
<head>
</head>
<body> ... </body>
</html>
```

The DOCTYPE is simply a statement about the allowed syntax or grammar used to layout the Web page. Basically, it says that the syntax is XHTML (which is almost identical to HTML 4.01). This is important information for the browser, which needs to be able to distinguish between XHTML and XML; it does this by checking the DOCTYPE.

There are currently three possible DOCTYPEs in XHTML: strict, transitional, or frameset. They are coded as follows:

Strict

```
<!DOCTYPE html PUBLIC "-//W3C//DTD XHTML 1.0
Strict//EN" "http://www.w3.org/TR/xhtml1/DTD/
xhtml1-strict.dtd">
```

This is saying that XHTML should be used for marking up the data and CSS used for presentation. No inline presentation tags, such as <font> or <b>, should be used.

Transitional

```
<!DOCTYPE html PUBLIC "-//W3C//DTD XHTML 1.0
Transitional//EN" "http://www.w3.org/TR/xhtml1/DTD/
xhtml-transitional.dtd">
```

This is the DOCTYPE used most typically as it permits CSS, tables, and inline fonts.

Frameset

```
<!DOCTYPE html PUBLIC "-//W3C//DTD XHTML 1.0
Frameset//EN" "http://www.w3.org/TR/xhtml1/DTD/
xhtml-frameset.dtd">
```

This DOCTYPE is used when the browser window is to be partitioned into two or more frames.

Namespace

In XHTML, a namespace attribute is typically added to the <html> tag or element. For example:

```
<html xmlns="http://www.w3.org/1999/xhtml">
```

Namespaces let you match a tag that you are using with a particular set of tags or elements. Namespaces play more of a role in XML where you might want to use the same tag or element with different meanings. For example, you might have a tag or element called *Description* referring to a product and a tag or element called *Description* referring to a place. A namespace refers to the scope or context in which a tag or element name is unique (it typically connects the tag or element to a specific DTD). A namespace is like a file system in which two files could both be named me.txt as long as they are stored in separate folders. Or, it is like two phone numbers that are identical, but are used to call different cities. By including the area code, you can uniquely identify which city you are calling. Or, it is like there being three people called John. They are uniquely identified by their surname: John Smith, John White, or John Black. In the case of an XHTML web page, the namespace state-ment is simply once again referencing the tags or elements used for XHTML (essentially the same as used in HTML 4.01).

Element and Attribute Names in Lowercase

XHTML element (or tag) and attribute names must be written in lowercase. Attribute values can be written in either upper- or lower-case. For example, "#ffcc33" can also be written as "#FFCC33."

Elements Must Nest with No Overlapping

Elements (or tags) must be closed in reverse order (i.e., last opened—first closed). For example:

```
<p>Be <b>Linda<b></p>
```

All Nonempty Elements Must Be Closed

In HTML, it is not essential to close, for example, the <p> tag, or the <td> or <tr> tags, or the <img> tag. These are nonempty tags (or elements), as they typically contain content. They each have a close tag, but it is often not used. In XHTML all tags or elements must be closed, explicitly or implicitly. For example:

```
<p>First paragraph</p> explicitly closed
<img src = "ulster.gif" /> implicitly closed using
the trailing forward slash before the end bracket
```

Empty Elements Must Be Terminated

Empty elements, or tags, have no content. So while a <p> element or tag contains a paragraph, a <br> element or tag is empty because it never contains anything. Another example is the <hr> tag or element.

In HTML, empty tags or elements do not have a closing tag. In XHTML, all empty elements must use the empty tag syntax, which is a trailing forward slash (/) before the end bracket. For example, <br> becomes <br /> and <hr> becomes <hr />. Note the space between the tag or element text and the />. This is for compatibility with current browsers.

Stand-Alone Attributes Must Be Expanded

In HTML, an attribute is minimized when there is only one possible value. For example:

```
<td nowrap>text</td>
<input type="checkbox" checked>
```

In XHTML, stand-alone attributes must be expanded. So, the above examples are written as follows:

```
<td nowrap="nowrap">text</td>
<input type="checkbox" checked="checked" />
```

Other popular attributes that are no longer stand-alone are selected and multiple (used with option in forms), noresize used with frames, and noshade used with the horizontal ruler tag.

The Id Attribute Replaces the Name Attribute

HTML 4.01 defines a name attribute for many tags or elements. It is excellent practice to give a name to as many tags or elements as possible, especially if you are using JavaScript. In XHTML the name attribute is deprecated and replaced with id. However, since current browsers are generally lagging behind new standards, it is best to use both name and id, with identical attribute values. For example:

```
<img src="goat.gif" id="goat" name="goat" />
```

Script and Style Elements

In XHTML the script and style elements must be prefaced as follows:

```
<script language="JavaScript"
type="text/javascript">
     <![CDATA[
          document.write("<b>Hello World!</b>");
     ]]>
     </script>
<style type="text/css">
     <![CDATA[
hr {color: sienna}
p {margin-left: 20px}
body {background-image: url("background.gif")}
     ]]>
</style>
</head>
```

It is not necessary to use CDATA if you are using either a self-contained JavaScript file ending in .js stored on the server or an external stylesheet file ending in .css stored on the server.

6

Using Dynamic XHTML: Graphics and JavaScript

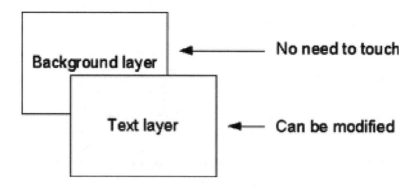

USING GRAPHICS INTELLIGENTLY

Website designers wishing to reach a global audience should avoid building graphics-intensive pages because these are slow to download. Many Internet users outside the United States have slow connections, and often they pay by the minute for Internet access. Also, when creating graphics, it is important to use a program like Photoshop that supports layers, which enable the website designer to use the same basic graphic design with different language versions of the site. The background of the graphic goes into one layer. Words in specific languages can be placed on several other different text layers and added to the basic layer as needed. For example, the basic layer could contain a search button. Layer two could contain the

English word *Search*. Layer three could contain the French word *Réchercher*. And so on. Then, all one needs to do is add the appropriate layer to the basic layer. This is especially useful for accommodating the width of letters in cursive scripts like Arabic, Farsi, or Urdu. Figures 6.1 and 6.2 illustrate the technique. For instructions on working with layers in Photoshop see appendix 6A at the end of this chapter.

TURNING TEXT INTO GRAPHICS

It is possible to position text on top of a graphic by using a style command. For example:

```
<img src = "picture.gif" width = "100" height =
"100">
<span style = "position: relative; top: -50;
left:-90; width: 80">Words of text</span>
```

There is, however, sometimes an advantage to turning the text into a graphic: A web browser will then display the text as it displays any graphic. It no longer matters that the original is in, for example, Korean. This approach can be useful if you need to give instructions to your user and you are unsure if he or she is using a version of a web

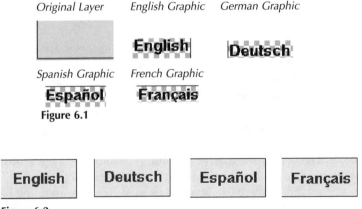

Figure 6.1

Figure 6.2

browser that will download the correct language fonts. See, for example, The Open Road Web Site set up by the State Library of Victoria at www.openroad.vic.gov.au, where instructions on configuring browsers are presented as graphics.

It is important to remember that turning text into graphics is the digital equivalent of photographing a word-processing file. The content is no longer text and cannot be changed by word processing software or an HTML editor. The only way to make a change is to go back to the original word-processing file, make the changes, and then resave the file as a graphic. For instructions on saving text as a graphic using Photoshop, see appendix 6B at the end of this chapter.

USING JAVASCRIPT TO IMPROVE ACCESS
FOR AN INTERNATIONAL AUDIENCE

JavaScript, VBScript, ColdFusion, Python, PHP, and ASP[1] are all web programming languages. JavaScript and VBScript are client-side programming languages. This means that the programming instructions are typically embedded into the web page as plain text. The instructions travel with the HTML or XHTML code to the user's computer and are executed by a JavaScript- or VBScript-compliant browser in the same way that the browser interprets HTML or XHTML tags.

ColdFusion, Python, PHP, and ASP are server-side technologies that can be used to display dynamic content on a web page. In these cases, the server must shoulder the processing burden of creating the pages for the user. The website designer must have access to the server and understand the programming languages.

Kenneth Tibbetts, in an article entitled "Why Script?"[2] points out the advantages of using a client-side programming language like JavaScript. He stresses that doing some of the work on the visitor's machine saves a lot of back-and-forth traffic. This is important when trying to reach a multinational audience whose bandwidth may be limited. He also argues that building in client-side programming (often called scripting) on a web page can make the difference between a usable page and a useful page. He points out that with scripting you can display exactly the information your visitor wants to focus on and easily change the view. Scripting can improve the users experience once the page is on his or her computer.

JavaScript: Quick Overview

JavaScript is an object-oriented programming language. When inserted onto a web page it works with HTML (and XHTML) to control different aspects of the page. JavaScript is a client-side interpreted language as opposed to a compiled language like Java. This means that the JavaScript programming instructions are either embedded into the XHTML document as plain text or called into the XHTML page from an external text file with the extension .js (in the same way that an external stylesheet is called into a web page). The programming instructions travel with the XHTML code to the user's computer, and the browser executes the instructions in the same way that the browser interprets XHTML tags.

JavaScript can increase user interactivity with a web page by, for example, prompting a user to fill in all or specific fields on a form or by helping a user locate suitable plug-ins. It does this by viewing the web page as a collection of objects. An easier way to think of this is in terms of the end product of each XHTML tag. Think of the <form> . . . </form> tag not in terms of the actual tag or element, but in terms of the object that is created, namely a form. Think of <img> in terms of the actual image that appears; a (as in <a href>) in terms of an actual link; <input type = "button"> in terms of a button; and so on. This collection of objects on a web page is seen by JavaScript as being in a hierarchy, with the window (or browser) at the top, followed by the document (or web page), and then the various objects on the web page (see figure 6.3). Some objects, such as the form object, contain other objects, such as text boxes, radio buttons, check boxes, select lists, and so on. JavaScript is trained to follow the hierarchy so that it can find particular objects on the web page and manipulate them according to programming instructions. By manipulating the different objects, we are able to manipulate the different parts of the web page.

Objects are generally manipulated by event handlers, which begin with on and are usually found in the body of the page. An event handler controls the user's interaction with the object. When the user performs an action, such as clicking the mouse button, he or she is really starting up an event handler. The event handler in its turn calls a function, which is a list of instructions executed whenever the event handler calls the function. The instructions might be

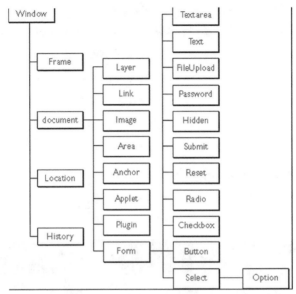

Figure 6.3   JavaScript Object Hierarchy

to go to another page or to ensure that data is entered into a form field or to open a pop-up window containing more information. JavaScript functions and the programming instructions they include can either go inside the head tag of the web page or be contained in a separate file (ending in .js) and called into the web page. A function name is always followed by parentheses: for example, function display().

Using Rollovers with Graphics

A rollover is an effect in which one image is replaced by another when the user moves the mouse pointer over it. This can be an effective way to offer language translations as the following examples demonstrate.

In the first example, various phrases appear in Spanish. They are actually graphics. When the user moves the mouse over a phrase, another graphic appears. The second graphic provides a translation of the Spanish phrase (see figures 6.4 and 6.5).

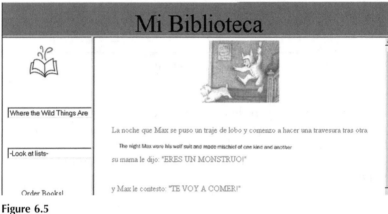

Mi Biblioteca

Where the Wild Things Are

-Look at lists-

Order Books!

La noche que Max se puso un traje de lobo y comenzo a hacer una travesura tras otra

su mama le dijo: "ERES UN MONSTRUO!"

y Max le contesto: "TE VOY A COMER!"

Figure 6.4

Mi Biblioteca

Where the Wild Things Are

-Look at lists-

Order Books!

La noche que Max se puso un traje de lobo y comenzo a hacer una travesura tras otra

The night Max wore his wolf suit and made mischief of one kind and another

su mama le dijo: "ERES UN MONSTRUO!"

y Max le contesto: "TE VOY A COMER!"

Figure 6.5

AUTUMN LANDSCAPE

Drop by drop rain slaps the banana leaves.
Praise whoever sketched this desolate scene:

the lush, dark canopies of the gnarled trees,
the long river, sliding smooth and white.

I lift my wine flask, drunk with rivers and hills.
My backpack, breathing moonlight, sags with poems.

Look, and love everyone.
Whoever sees this landscape is stunned.

Figure 6.6

Cảnh Thu

Thánh thót tẩu tiêu mấy hạt mưa,
Khen ai khéo vẽ cảnh tiêu sơ.
Xanh om cổ thụ tròn xoe tán,
Trắng xoá tràng giang phẳng lặng tờ
Bầu dốc giang sơn say chấp rượu,
Túi lưng phong nguyệt nặng vì thơ.
Ơ hay, cảnh cũng ưa người nhỉ,
Ai thấy, ai mà chẳng ngẩn ngơ

Figure 6.7 *Source:* pacificrimvoices.org/
regionalpages/aug00issue/vietpoetry.html

In the second example, when the user moves the mouse over the English poem, a Vietnamese translation follows (see figures 6.6 and 6.7). The XHTML code and JavaScript that make this rollover work can be found at senna.sjsu.edu/lmain/global/ rollover.html and in appendix 6C at the end of this chapter "Rollover.html". Note the use of /*....*/ to insert comments inside a JavaScript program.

Automatic Direction from a Drop Down List

JavaScript can take the choice from the pull down menu built in chapter 5 and automatically return different pages according to the selection made by the user (see figure 6.8). When the user makes a selection from the drop down list, the onChange event handler starts up a function called formhandler, which is stored in the page's <head> tag. This function contains lines of programming that tell the browser to put the URL associated with the selection in the location box of the browser, and the page in the correct language is brought up. The XHTML code and JavaScript that make this function work can be found at senna.sjsu.edu/lmain/ global/listopen.html and in appendix 6C at the end of this chapter ("Menus.html").

Figure 6.8

Using JavaScript to Change Stylesheets

The page at senna.sjsu.edu/lmain/global/changestylesheets. html illustrates JavaScript working with XHTML and CSS to enable the user to change the webpage interface (see figures 6.9 and 6.10). Each stylesheet can be tailored to a specific culture. The code is also listed in appendix 6C at the end of this chapter ("Changestylesheets.html").

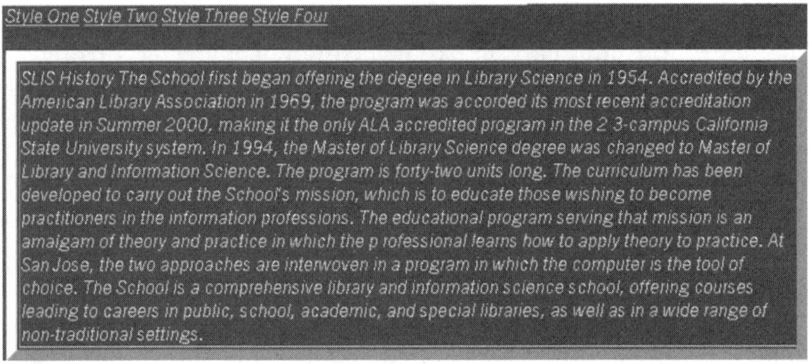

Figure 6.9

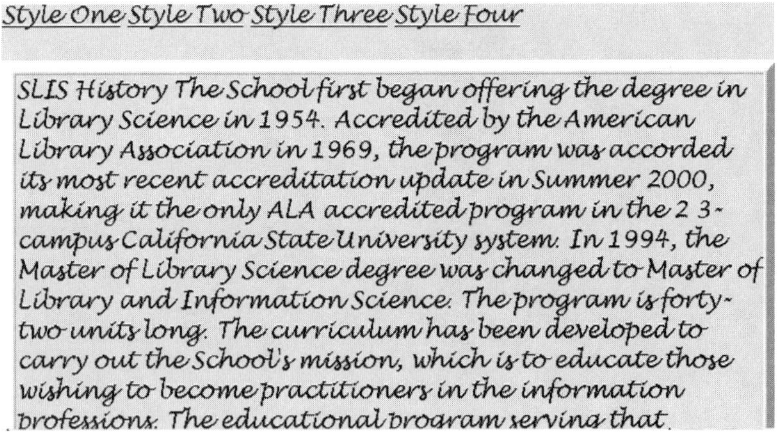

Figure 6.10

Using Cookies to Assist with Language Choice

As mentioned in chapter 2, it is possible to ascertain the language in which the user prefers to view the web page and store that information in a cookie. Cookies are small computer-generated text files that are sent to the user's computer. They store information on that computer for retrieval in later browsing sessions. So when the user returns to the page, his or her browser will automatically bring up the page in the correct language. This will fail, of course, if the user moves to a different computer or if the cookie file is deleted. For example, the menu shown in figure 6.11 will only appear the first time a user comes to the page. On subsequent visits this menu will not appear, and the page in the selected language will appear. The code to make this work can be found at senna.sjsu.edu/lmain/global/cookieschinese.html.

To work with cookies, the programmer must code three functions into the Web page: one to read the cookie, one to store information in the cookie, and one to delete the cookie. When the user makes a selection, the event handler onClick, which stores the name of the language in a cookie, is called. If the name of the language is, for example, German, then the page german.html comes up. If the name of the language selected is Spanish, then the page spanish.html comes up. The browser checks the cookie for this information the next time the user visits that website. For a good explanation of cookies, see www.echoecho.com/jscookies.htm.

Using JavaScript to Read the Language of the User's Browser

JavaScript can detect the localized language version of the user's browser (this is separate from having the web page coded in a certain language or using a certain charset). It does this by recording a language code using the ISO 639 language codes (discussed in chap-

        ⌐ English
        ⌐ Français
        ⌐ Deutsch
        ⌐ Español
        ⌐ Português
        ⌐ 中文

Figure 6.11

ter 2). This information can be used to automatically take a user to
the correct language page (see figure 6.12). The assumption is that
the user's language of preference will be the same as the language of
his or her browser. One, of course, needs separate pages in different
languages. The code for this function can be found at senna.
sjsu.edu/lmain/global/selectinglanguage.html and in appendix 6C
at the end of this chapter ("Selectinglanguage.html").

JavaScript discovers the language of the user's browser and
stores that language code in a variable[3] called m_lang (var m_lang =
navigator.browserLanguage). Then a series of checks are run. The
first check looks to see if the content of m_lang is de (code for
German). If it is, then Javascript places german.html in the
browser's location box (the place in the browser where the URL is
entered). Checks are run for en-us (United States English), nl
(Dutch), and ja (Japanese). Notice the use of the double equals (==).
This is the JavaScript comparison operator. Nothing is being
changed; two things are merely being examined, namely the content
of m_lang to see if it contains the letters de or en-us, and so on. Notice also that the program runs automatically when the user acti-
vates this Web page. The program uses a system event handler
called onLoad, which is placed in the <body> tag or element. As
soon as the page loads into the user's computer, the function
browser() (which performs the above task) is automatically called.

The same technique can also be used to bring up a message to a
user in his or her language that says that the web content is not
available in his or her language. For example, the website is in English with pages available in German, Italian, Portuguese, and Spanish. JavaScript detects that the user has a French browser. The page
shown in figure 6.13 will come up. Another example might be that
JavaScript detects that the user's browser is in English while the
website content is in French with pages available in German, Italian,
Portuguese, and Spanish. The message contained in figure 6.14
might appear.

Welcome to the Web Site

This is the English language Web page. The Web Site is also available in the following languages.

Français Deutsch Русский Português Español

Figure 6.12

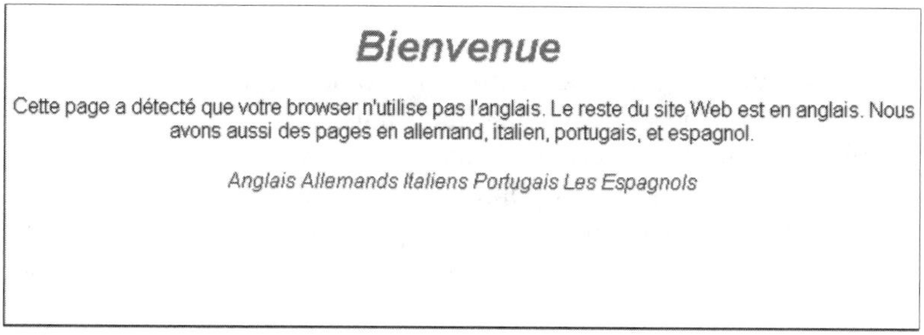

Bienvenue

Cette page a détecté que votre browser n'utilise pas l'anglais. Le reste du site Web est en anglais. Nous avons aussi des pages en allemand, italien, portugais, et espagnol.

Anglais Allemands Italiens Portugais Les Espagnols

Figure 6.13

Welcome to the Web Site

This page has detected that your browser is using English. The Web Site is in French with some pages in German, Italian, Portuguese,and Spanish.

French German Italian Portuguese Spanish

Figure 6.14

If you do not wish to have message pages available for all languages, it is possible to have a default message appear if the user's browser language does not correspond to any of the languages of the message pages. For this to work correctly, the names of the XHTML language pages must correspond to the names of the language codes. You can have message pages in any language that you wish as long as you name them using the ISO 639 language codes (discussed in chapter 2). This version of the program can be found at senna.sjsu.edu/lmain/global/browserlanguage.html and in appendix 6C at the end of this chapter ("Browserlanguage.html"). The language code is stored in the variable or electronic envelope called code. If the content of the variable code is one of the listed names, then that name is sent back to the function showpage(). The showpage() function contains instructions to open a subwindow within the main screen, add .html to the language code name of the browser detected by JavaScript, and insert an HTML page that begins either with fr (French), de (German), it (Italian), es (Spanish), pt (Portuguese), or en (English). If the language of the user's browser does not match any of the listed languages, then a web page called default is displayed.

Pop-Up Windows

Pop-up windows can be useful for providing immediate help or
feedback. For instance, you could have a list of languages, and when
the user clicks the appropriate language, a window with information in that language could pop up (see figures 6.15 to 6.17).

There are two ways to code pop-up windows. The code can be
found at senna.sjsu.edu/lmain/global/japanchinahint.html and

Japan

Simplified Chinese

Figure 6.15

Figure 6.16

Japanese

Simplified Chinese

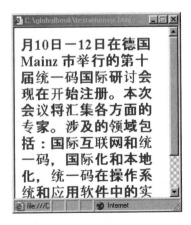

Figure 6.17

senna.sjsu.edu/lmain/global/jp.html and in appendix 6C at the end of this chapter ("Japanchinahint.html" and "Jp.html"). In japanchinahint.html, when the user clicks on Japanese, the function verifyj() is activated. This function opens up a smaller window and composes an XHTML document complete with the correct charset. The same thing happens when the user clicks on the simplified Chinese option. This time function verifycn() is called, also with the correct charset. Note how to configure a pop-up window. You basically make it a big variable by giving it a name (e.g., layout and layout1). Then you say window.open and, in this example, use the JavaScript document.write command to create an XHTML page.

It is also possible to create a pop-up window and simply call a previously written XHTML document into the window as is done in jp.html, which calls japanpop-up.html into the newly created window (see figure 6.18). Note that in this case, you start by saying which XHTML document will display in the pop-up window (in this case japanpop-up.html). Then you give the pop-up window a name. Next you configure its appearance. Note the punctuation here. You start by saying how wide and how tall it will be, followed by its position on the screen. Then decide if you want a menu bar (file, edit, etc.), a toolbar (back, forward, stop, etc.), a location box, a status bar, a directories bar (the one with the bookmarks), or scrollbars. You can also set resizable to no or yes. Nancy Hickman gives an example of using a pop-up window to display metric and inches and the ability to switch between them.[4]

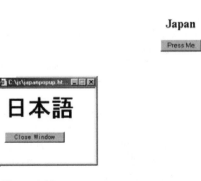

Figure 6.18

Forms

A form enables a user to send information back to you and makes the World Wide Web—and your XHTML document—a truly interactive environment. In a form, the reader can type in information or make choices using radio buttons or check boxes. However, working with forms involves not only designing the form as part of your HTML or XHTML document, but also writing scripts that will be stored on the server. These server scripts are typically written in a language called practical extraction and report language (Perl) or in C++. They contain instructions as to what the server software is to do with the data it receives from the user via the form. Scripts are usually stored in a directory called the cgi-bin. The letters *cgi* stand for common gateway interface, which is essentially a protocol, or set of software rules, that enables forms to communicate with the programs or scripts that process them. Cgi directories do not have to be called cgi-bin, but they must begin with *cgi*.

It is important to understand conceptually what happens when a form is executed on the web. There are three main stages:

1. A user enters data into the form.
2. The data are stored in what are called memory variables. A memory variable is an area of random access memory (RAM) set aside to hold input from a user. These memory variables are defined in the form interface, and each input option in the form has a memory variable associated with it. We sometimes think of variables as electronic envelopes.
3. The browser transfers the data in the memory variables to the server software, which in turn transfers the data to a cgi directory on the server. The cgi directory contains a script or program that receives the data and performs an action on it, such as storing it in a file until someone is ready use it (e.g., fill an order, find information, process the results of a survey).

After the script in the cgi directory processes the data, a response is usually sent back to the user confirming receipt of an order or thanking him or her for the input. It is important to make sure that the response is in the correct language. A Korean user should not be thanked in English. In addition, the correct charset must be specified. Text input into a form reaches the cgi program in the charset of the local machine rather than that of the web page. The correct charset should be added as an attribute in the <form> tag or element. For example:

```
<form action="/cgi-main/gform" method = "post"
accept-charset="iso-8859-1,UTF-8">
```

This attribute specifies the list of character encodings for input data accepted by the server processing this form. The value is a space- or comma-delimited list of charset values. The charset attribute can also be added to the <input> and <textarea> tags or elements.

So where does JavaScript fit in? JavaScript runs checks on the data input by the user—and it does so in the user's computer. Only after all the checks are complete will JavaScript permit the browser to send the envelopes or variables to the server. So JavaScript works client-side; cgi processing is conducted server-side.

JavaScript, of course, views the form as a collection of objects on the page. The form interface shown in figure 6.19 illustrates how that Web page is really a collection of objects, almost all of which are part of the form object. This form object has two text box objects, one radio button object made up of three radio buttons,[5] three check box objects, one text area object, and one drop down list object (called a select object). All these things are objects in their own right, but they are objects considered to be "under" the form object. Variables (electronic envelopes) are attached to the objects. The user's selection or input is stored in the variable, and when the user presses the send button (the submit object), JavaScript steps in to make whatever checks on the user's input the form designer requested. Typical checks might include ensuring that certain fields are filled in or certain features are present in the data, such as an @ symbol in an e-mail address. After the JavaScript program has completed its checks, the envelopes or variables are sent to the server—specifically, to a cgi directory on the server. Once there, the contents of the envelopes are processed by whichever program is so stated in the action attribute of the <form> tag.

Enter Your Name: [   ]

Enter Your E-Mail Address: [   ]

The home page design was: ⊂ Good ⊂ OK ⊂ Awful

What was your favourite activity on the island? | Fishing ⌃ |
| Diving |
| Bird Watching ⌄ |

Would you like more information on our services by: ⌐ Mail ⌐ E-Mail ⌐ Phone

Enter Your Comments in the Space Provided Here: [   ]

[Send] [Clear]

Figure 6.19

Figure 6.20 provides an example of a form developed for an international audience. Although the form shown is written in English, the website may have a variety of forms written in different languages. Messages in alert boxes in forms should, of course, correspond to the language of the parent form. Note the following points:

1. The user is required to enter his or her family name, city, phone, and e-mail address. The user is also required to make a selection from one of the radio buttons and one of the check boxes and to select a country from the drop down list. In addition, if the shipping address and the billing address are the same, the program will transfer the address for the user.
2. The terms *family name* and *given name* are used, and plenty of space is provided for the user to enter the name.
3. Three address lines are used in order to accommodate various address formats.
4. State, province, and prefecture are used, instead of just state.
5. The term postal code is used instead of zip code.
6. The form provides a list of countries. When the user selects a country, the selection is automatically placed in a text box. The

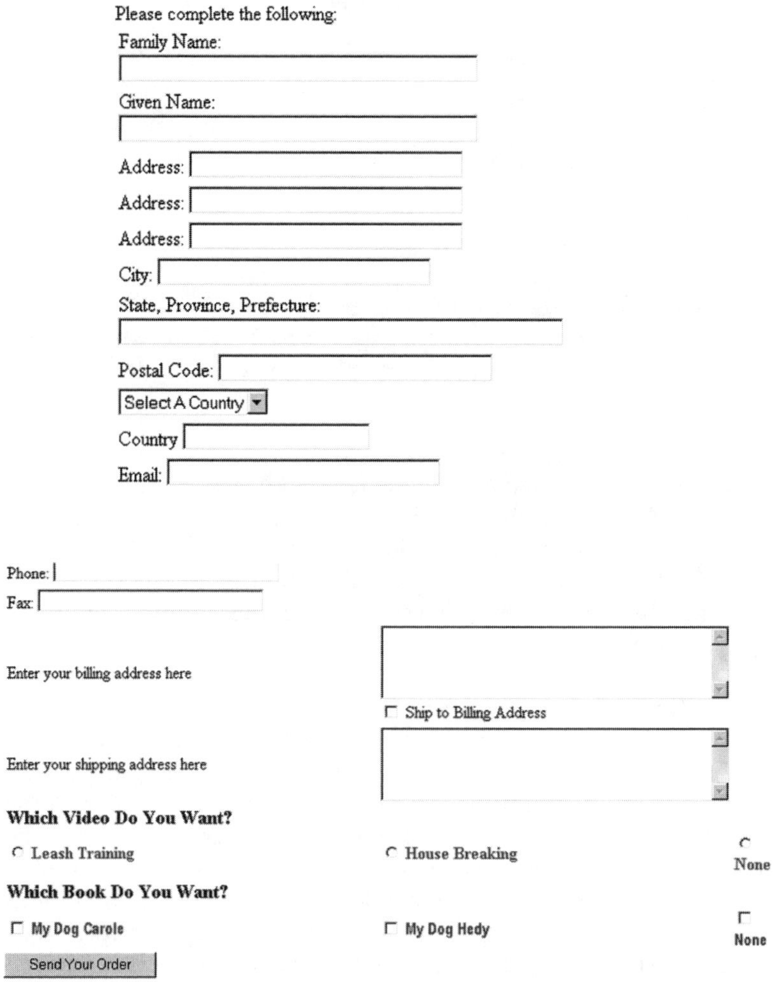

Please complete the following:
Family Name:

Given Name:

Address:

Address:

Address:

City:

State, Province, Prefecture:

Postal Code:

Select A Country ▾

Country

Email:

Phone:

Fax:

Enter your billing address here

☐ Ship to Billing Address

Enter your shipping address here

Which Video Do You Want?

○ Leash Training ○ House Breaking ○ None

Which Book Do You Want?

☐ My Dog Carole ☐ My Dog Hedy ☐ None

Send Your Order

Figure 6.20

list should be in the language initially selected by the user when entering the site (see figure 6.21a and b).

7. The form checks that an e-mail address entered contains an @ symbol, a period, no spaces, and is at least six characters long. This permits some checking on the format of the e-mail address input by the user but should still accommodate all e-mails address formats (see figure 6.22).

Figure 6.21a and b

Figure 6.22

8. The form checks that only the following characters are used in the phone field: 0123456789()–+ (see figure 6.23). (See the discussion of phone numbers in chapter 3).
9. If the form is used to perform calculations, it is important to remember that taxes will vary tremendously from country to country.

The form shown in figure 6.20 can be seen at senna.sjsu. edu/lmain/global/en_jsformint.html and in appendix 6C at the end of this chapter ("En_jsformint.html" and "En_jsint.js").The JavaScript programming instructions are stored in a separate file called en_jsint.js, which is called into the web page. This technique makes it easy to have a series of forms in different languages all saved as separate .js files and is in keeping with the building-block approach to website design. Indeed, all JavaScript programs can be saved as external files (ending in .js, as in the form example). The relevant language.js file can then be called into the web page. It is easy to add new .js files or make changes to a particular .js file. It is cru-

Figure 6.23

cial to remember to change all message boxes, alert messages, error messages, and the like into the appropriate language. Note the way in which all the parts of the form (the various objects that make up the form) are named. Also note the event handlers (starting with *on*) that activate the various functions coded in en_jsint.js. Further comments are scattered throughout the program.

Figures 6.24 to 6.28 illustrate another way to handle country selection. State options only come up if the United States is selected. Province options come up for Canada, and region options come up for the United Kingdom. The website designer could set up similar options for other countries. The code can be found at senna.sjsu.edu/lmain/global/testform.html.

Figure 6.24

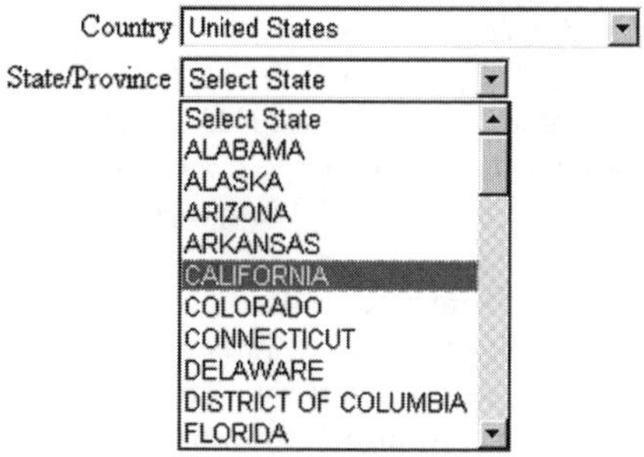

Figure 6.25

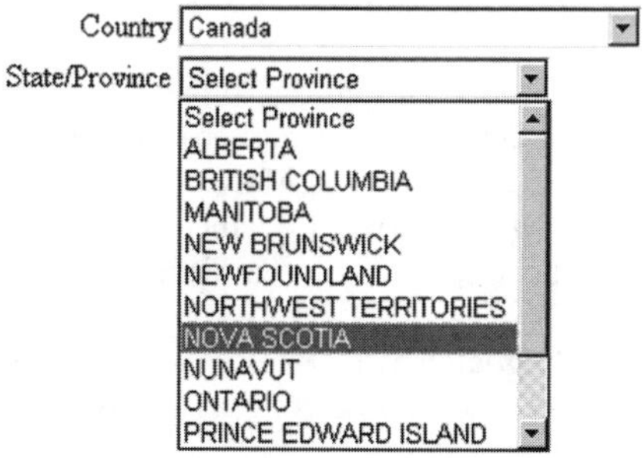

Figure 6.26

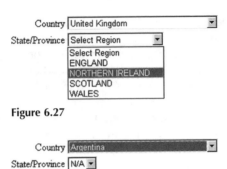

Figure 6.27

Figure 6.28

NOTES

1. Active Server Pages (ASP) in itself is not a language. It uses VBScript (based on Visual Basic) or JavaScript to display dynamic content. ASP typically runs on a Microsoft server but can be run from other platforms using Chili!Soft.asp (http://www.chilisoft.com).

2. Kenneth Tibbetts, "Why Script?" *WebReference Newsletter,* March 28, 2002, at www.webreference.com/new/020328.html (accessed March 1, 2002).

3. A memory variable is an area of RAM (random access memory) set aside to hold input from a user. A variable can be thought of as an electronic envelope.

4. Nancy Hickman, "Internationalizing Your Web Site" at www.webtechniques.com/archives/1998/03/junk (accessed March 1, 2002).

5. Since a user can only select one from a grouping of radio buttons (they are mutually exclusive), each grouping of radio buttons is a single object.

REFERENCES

Kaplan, Michael. "Go Global: Designing Your ASP-Based Web Site to Support Globalization," 2000, at msdn.microsoft.com/msdnmag/issues/0700/localize/localize.asp (accessed March 1, 2002).

Melnick, Jim. "Multilingual Forms in Unicode" at www-106.ibm.com/developerworks/unicode/library/os-mult.html?dwzone=unicode (accessed March 1, 2002).

"Unicode-based Multilingual Form Development" at www6.software.ibm.com/developerworks/education/u-concept/index.html (accessed March 1, 2002).

APPENDIX 6A: WORKING
WITH LAYERS IN PHOTOSHOP

If you add anything to an image, such as text or artwork, Photoshop automatically creates a new layer. This is a very useful feature because the addition does not become a permanent part of your image until you merge the layers. In fact, each item that you add to the image should be kept in its own layer until you are ready to merge them together. You can draw, edit, paste, and reposition things on a layer without disturbing any other layer.

After opening Photoshop, select *File/New* (see figure 6.29).

Figure 6.29

A box will open up on the screen. Make sure that the box is sized as you want it. Select *Image/Image Size*. In the following examples, the boxes are 122 × 59 px (see figure 6.30).

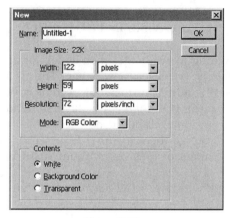

Figure 6.30

Make sure the layers palette is visible. Select *Windows/Show Layers* (see figure 6.31).

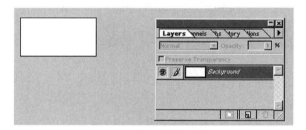

Figure 6.31

Select *Image/Mode/RGB Color* (see figure 6.32).

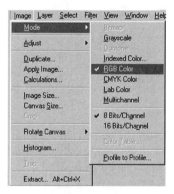

Figure 6.32

Select the background and foreground colors by clicking on the squares with the arrows in the tool box on the left (if the tool box is not visible, select *Window/Show Tools*). Select the desired colors (see figure 6.33).

Figure 6.33

Select *Layer/New/Layer* (see fig-ure 6.34).

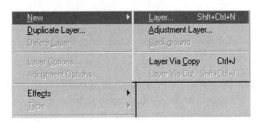

Figure 6.34

Click in the *Name* box to give the layer a name (for example, *back*). Look in the *Mode* box. Make sure that *Normal* is selected (see figure 6.35).

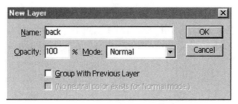

Figure 6.35

Repeat the above steps to create a second layer. Give the second layer a name, such as *englishtext*. In this case the *Mode* box should show *Multiply* (see figure 6.36).

Figure 6.36

Repeat for as many layers as you need (see figure 6.37).

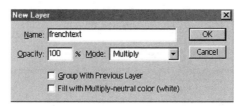

Figure 6.37

Edit one layer at a time. The layer being edited is the active layer. Select it by clicking on the layer to highlight its name. A little paintbrush icon will appear. To work on another layer, click on its name to make it the active layer. Add foreground color to a layer by pressing alt and backspace. To fill the background with color, press ctrl and backspace.

To type, click the text tool (the *T* in the tool box). Click where you want the text to display. The *Type Tool* box appears (see figure 6.38).

Type in the text field where the cursor is flashing. Notice the options to select font, point size, leading (space between lines of type), spacing (space between characters), and attributes, like bold and alignment. Selecting *Anti-Alias* removes sharp edges from letter forms but increases the size of the file.

Figure 6.38

To delete a highlighted layer, click on the trash can in the layer palette or select *Layer/Delete Layer.* When merging layers, make sure that each layer to be merged has an eyeball showing. Then, select *Layer/Merge Down* or *Flatten Image.*

Filters

To add special effects with filters, click the background in the layers palette to make it active. Select, for example, *Filter/Brush Strokes/Sprayed Strokes,* then click *OK.* This filter adds brush strokes to the background. Select *Filter/Artistic/Rough Pastels* to make the background look as if it were drawn with pastel chalks. These are just two examples; there are many other choices.

APPENDIX 6B: SAVING TEXT AS
A GRAPHIC IN PHOTOSHOP

Open Photoshop and select *File/New/Paste*. Paste the text from the word-processing document (see figure 6.39).

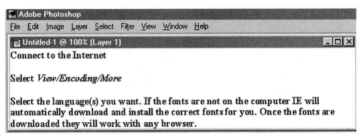

Figure 6.39

Select *Image/Mode/RGB Color*. When prompted to flatten, confirm (see figure 6.40).

Figure 6.40

Then select *File/Save As* and choose either .GIF or .JPG (see figure 6.41)

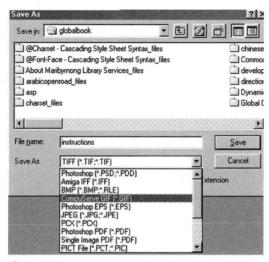

Figure 6.41

The GIF format is best for graphics that look like text (see figure 6.42) and text art, poster art, icons, or buttons. Programs such as Photoshop also contain a *Save for the Web* feature that will optimize the colors in the graphic and reduce the file size, improving download time.

Connect to the Internet

Select *View/Encoding/More*

Select the language(s) you want. If the fonts are not on the computer IE will automatically download and install the correct fonts for you. Once the fonts are downloaded they will work with any browser.

Figure 6.42

Since the text presented in figure 6.42 is now a graphic, it should be coded as such in the XHTML web page. As with any graphic, alt, width, and height attributes should be added.

APPENDIX 6C: JAVASCRIPT CODE

Rollover.html

```
<!DOCTYPE html PUBLIC "-//W3C//DTD XHTML 1.0
Transitional//EN" "http://www.w3.org/TR/xhtml1/DTD/xhtml1
-transitional.dtd">
<html xmlns="http://www.w3.org/1999/xhtml" lang="en-US"
xml:lang="en-US" dir="ltr">
<head>
<title>Rollover</title>
<meta http-equiv="content-type" content="text/html;
charset=UTF-8" />
<head>
<title>Rollover</title>
<script language="JavaScript">
<!--
```

The following preloads the images into the cache directory on the user's computer. This will make the rollovers work faster. You create an image object for each image, specifying its width and height (which you will obtain from a graphics program), and give the object a name. In the example below, the image objects are called image01 and image02. Then you feed in the name and extension of the image. The if(document. images) statement checks that a user is working with a level 3 or higher browser. Earlier browsers are not capable of preloading images in this fashion.

```
if(document.images)
image01 = new Image(250,250)
image01.src="auteng.gif"
image02= new Image(250,250)
image02.src="autviet.gif"
 //-->
 </script>
 </head>
<body bgcolor = "white">
```

The rollover happens in the following code. Notice that everything is wrapped within the open (<) and close (>) tag signs (including the image that appears on the page when the page first loads). The href attribute is set to "#"*, as the browser should not actually follow a URL. The word *example* is the name of the image that first appears on the screen. Do not confuse the name of the image (example) with the name of the image file (auteng.gif). If you have more than one image on the web page, make sure that each image has its own name (example, example1, and so on).

```
<a href="#" onmouseover="document.images['example'].
src=image02.src"
onmouseout= "document.images['example'].src=image01.
src">
<img src="auteng.gif" height = "250" width = "250"
name="example" id = "example" border = "0"></a>
</body>
</html>
```

Menus.html

```
<!DOCTYPE html PUBLIC "-//W3C//DTD XHTML 1.0
Transitional//EN""http://www.w3.org/TR/xhtml1/DTD/xht
ml1-transitional.dtd">
<html xmlns="http://www.w3.org/1999/xhtml" lang="en-
US" xml:lang="en-US" dir="ltr">
<head>
<meta http-equiv="content-type" content="text/html;
charset=UTF-8" />
<link rel="stylesheet" type="text/css"
href="langlinks.css" />
<title>Language Choice with Javascript</title>
<script language="javaScript">
<!—hide
function formhandler()
{
var urlbox1=
document.one.langlinks.options[document.one.langlinks
.selectedIndex].value; window.location.href = urlbox1
}
//end hide—>
</script>
</head>
<body bgcolor="ffffff">
<form name = "one">
<select name="langlinks" id = "langlinks" onChange =
"formhandler()" size = "10">
<option value="ru.html" />&#1056;&#1091;&#1089;&#1089;
&#1082;&#1080;&#1081;
```

```
<option value="hk.html" />&#20013;&#25991; (HK)
</option>
<option value="cn.html" />&#20013;&#25991; (CN)
</option>
<option value="fr.html" />Fran&ccedil;ais</option>
<option value = "en.html" />English</option>
<option value = "pt.html" />Portugu&ecirc;s
</option>
<option value = "ro.html" />Rom&acirc;n&#259;</option>
<option value = "tu.html" />T&uuml;rk&ccedil;e</option>
<option value = "gr.html" />&#917;&#955;&#955;&#951;
&#957;&#953;&#954;&#940; (Ellynika)</option>
<option value = "es.html" />Espa&ntilde;ol</option>
</select>
</form>
</body>
</html>
```

Changestylesheets.html

```
<!DOCTYPE html PUBLIC "-//W3C//DTD XHTML 1.0
Transitional//EN""http://www.w3.org/TR/xhtml1/DTD/xht
ml1-transitional.dtd">
<html xmlns="http://www.w3.org/1999/xhtml" lang="en-
US" xml:lang="en-US" dir="ltr">
<head>
<meta http-equiv="content-type" content="text/html;
charset=UTF-8" />
```

Setting up the stylesheets. Create your stylesheets, and set the link rels up to load them as shown below. These belong in the <head> of the page. What you name the stylesheet files does not matter (so long as the extension is .css) because the script references them only by a number, not the file name. You can use as few or as many stylesheets as needed. The script will automatically detect the number of stylesheets in use. Note the order of the stylesheets. The last sheet loaded is the one the browser will use initially. One trick to avoid confusion is shown below, where the first sheet is loaded an additional time at the end of the list.

```
<link rel="stylesheet" href="style_1.css">
<link rel="stylesheet" href="style_2.css">
<link rel="stylesheet" href="style_3.css">
```

```
<link rel="stylesheet" href="style_4.css">
<link rel="stylesheet" href="style_1.css">
```

Setting up the JavaScript. . . . Insert the following script in the <head> of the page, usually right after the link rel's.

```
<script language="Javascript">
<!--hide
var doAlerts=false
function changeSheets(whichSheet){
 whichSheet=whichSheet-1
 if(document.styleSheets)
{
   var c = document.styleSheets.length;
   if (doAlerts) alert('Change to Style
'+(whichSheet+1))
   for(var i=0;i<c;i++)
{
    if(i!=whichSheet)
{
     document.styleSheets[i].disabled=true;
    }else{
     document.styleSheets[i].disabled=false;
    }
   }
  }
}
//end hide-->
</script>
</head>
<body>
<a href="JavaScript:changeSheets(1)">Style One</a>
<a href="JavaScript:changeSheets(2)">Style Two</a>
<a href="JavaScript:changeSheets(3)">Style Three</a>
<a href="JavaScript:changeSheets(4)">Style Four</a>
<!--Content -->
```

Selectinglanguage.html

```
<!DOCTYPE html PUBLIC "-//W3C//DTD XHTML 1.0
Transitional//EN" "http://www.w3.org/TR/xhtml1/DTD/xht
ml1-transitional.dtd">
<html xmlns="http://www.w3.org/1999/xhtml" lang="en-
US" xml:lang="en-US" dir="ltr">
```

```
<head>
<title>Different Languages</title>
<meta http-equiv="content-type" content="text/html;
charset=UTF-8" />
<script language="javascript">
Function browser()
{
  var m_browserName = navigator.appName;
  var m_userAgent = navigator.userAgent;
  var m_lang = navigator.browserLanguage

  if(m_lang == "de")
  {
    window.location.href = "german.html";
  }
  if(m_lang == "en-us")
  {
    window.location.href = "english.html";
  }
  if(m_lang == "nl")
  {
      window.location.href = "dutch.html";
  }
  if(m_lang == "ja")
  {
    window.location.href = "ja.html";
  }
  }
</script>
</head>
<body bgcolor="#999999" onLoad="browser()">
</body>
</html>
```

Browserlanguage.html

```
<!DOCTYPE html PUBLIC "-//W3C//DTD XHTML 1.0
Transitional//EN""http://www.w3.org/TR/xhtml1/DTD/xht
ml1-transitional.dtd">
<html xmlns="http://www.w3.org/1999/xhtml" lang="en-
US" xml:lang="en-US" dir="ltr">
<head>
<title>Language</title>
<meta http-equiv="content-type" content="text/html;
```

```
charset=UTF-8" />
<script language="JavaScript1.2">
<!--
```

You must specify to the browser to use JavaScript 1.2 or higher. The contents of the variable code are used inside this function.

```
function showpage(code)
  {
```

This instructs the browser to draw out a smaller window.

```
var Y = (screen.height - 400)/2;
  var X = (screen.width - 600)/2;
  msgWindow =
window.open('','targetName2','height=400,
width=600,screenX='+X+',screenY='+Y+',left='+X+',top=
'+Y);
```

This puts the content of the variable code with .html added into the location box of the newly created window.

```
msgWindow.location.href = code + '.html';
  }
if (navigator.appName == 'Netscape')
  var language = navigator.language;
else
  var language = navigator.browserLanguage;
```

JavaScript detects the language of the user's browser and inserts it into the variable code. If the language code is one of the following, then the appropriate page will display inside the window created by function showpage(). If not, then the page called default.html will come up.

```
var code = language.substring(0,2);
if (code == 'fr' || code == 'de' || code == 'it' ||
code == 'es' || code == 'pt' || code =='en')
  showpage(code);
else
  showpage('default');
</script>
</head>
</body>
</html>
```

Japanchinahint.html

```
<!DOCTYPE html PUBLIC "-//W3C//DTD XHTML 1.0
Transitional//EN""http://www.w3.org/TR/xhtml1/DTD/xht
ml1-transitional.dtd">
<html xmlns="http://www.w3.org/1999/xhtml" lang="en-
US" xml:lang="en-US" dir="ltr">
<head>
<meta http-equiv="content-type" content="text/html;
charset=UTF-8" />
<title>Opening Windows for Different Languages</title>
<script language = "javascript">
<!-hide
function verifyj()
{
layout=window.open("","target",'toolbar=no,location=n
o,directories=no,status=yes,menubar=no,scrollbars=yes
,resizable=no, width=280, height=280,left=385,
top=150');

layout.document.write("<html><head><meta http-equiv=\
"Content-Type\"content=\"text/html; charset =x-euc-
jp\" /></head><body bgcolor=\"#ffffff\"><a
href=\"#\"><h2><font face=\"Osaka\"><font size =
\+4\">&#26085;&#26412;&#35486; </font>
</h2><\/a>");
}
function verifycn()
{
layout1=window.open("","target",'toolbar=no,location=
no,directories=no,status=yes,menubar=no,scrollbars=ye
s,resizable=no, width=280, height=280,left=385,
top=150');

layout1.document.write("<html><head><meta http-
equiv=\"Content-Type\"content=\"text/html; charset
=GB2312\" /></head><body bgcolor=\"#ffffff\">
<a href=\"#\"><h2>æœ^10æ—¥¹/₄□12æ—¥åœ¨å³/₄·å›¹/₂ Mainz
å¸¸ä¸³/₄è¡Œçš„ç¬¬å□□å±Šç»Ÿä¸€ç □å›¹/₂é™…ç
"è®¨ä¹/₄šçŽºåœ¨ä¹/₄€å§<æ³¨å†Œã€,æœ¬æ¬¡ä¹/₄šè®®åº
†æ±‡é>†å□„æ–¹é□¢çš„ä¸"å®¶ã€,æ¶‰å□Šçš„é¢†åŸŸåŒ…æ
<¬ï¹/₄šå›¹/₂é™…åº ¨è□"ç¹/₂'å'Œç»Ÿä¸€ç □ï¹/₄Œå›¹/₂
é™…åŒ—å'Œæœ¬åœºåŒ-ï¹/₄Œç»Ÿä¸€ç
□åœ¨æ"□ä¹/₂œç³»ç»Ÿå'Œåº¨"ç""è¹/₂⁻ä»¶ä¸.-çš„å®žçŽºï¹/₄Œå--
```

```
åž<ï¹⁄₄Œæ-‡æœ¬æ  ¹⁄₄å¹⁄₄□ä»¥å□Šå□?šæ-‡ç§□è®¡ç®—ç?‰ã€,
</font></h2><\/a>");
}
//end hide-->
</script>
</head>
<body bgcolor="ffffff">
<a href = "#" onClick = "verifyj()">Japan</a><p>
<a href = "#" onClick = "verifycn()">Simplified
Chinese</a>
</body>
</html>
```

Jp.html

```
<!DOCTYPE html PUBLIC "-//W3C//DTD XHTML 1.0
Transitional//EN""http://www.w3.org/TR/xhtml1/DTD/xht
ml1-transitional.dtd">
<html xmlns="http://www.w3.org/1999/xhtml" lang="en-
US" xml:lang="en-US" dir="ltr">
<head>
<meta http-equiv="content-type" content="text/html;
charset=utf-8" />
<title></title>
<script language = "javascript">
function makewindow()
{
gallery=window.open("japanpopup.html","gallery",'tool
bar=no,directories=no,menubar=no,scrollbars=no,top=25
0,width=200,height=150');
}
</script>
</head>
<body bgcolor="#FFFFFF">
<p>
<center>
<h2>Japan</h2>
<p><form><input type = "button" name = "im" value =
"Press Me"
onClick = "makewindow()"></a></form>
</center>
</body>
</html>
```

Japanpopup.html

```
<!DOCTYPE html PUBLIC "-//W3C//DTD XHTML 1.0
Transitional//EN""http://www.w3.org/TR/xhtml1/DTD/xht
ml1-transitional.dtd">
<html xmlns="http://www.w3.org/1999/xhtml">
<head>
<meta http-equiv="content-type" content="text/html;
charset=x-euc-jp" />
<title></title>
</head>
<body bgcolor="ffffff">
<h2><font face="Osaka"><font size = "+4">&#26085;
&#26412;&#35486; </font></h2>
<form><input type = "button" value = "Close Window"
onClick = "self.close()">
</form>
</body>
</html>
```

En_jsformint.html

```
<!DOCTYPE html PUBLIC "-//W3C//DTD XHTML 1.0
Transitional//EN""http://www.w3.org/TR/xhtml1/DTD/xht
ml1-transitional.dtd">
<html xmlns="http://www.w3.org/1999/xhtml" lang="en-
US" xml:lang="en-US" dir="ltr">
<html xmlns="http://www.w3.org/1999/xhtml"
xml:lang="en-US" lang="en-US" dir = "ltr">
<head>
<title>Order Form</title>
<meta http-equiv="content-type" content="text/html;
charset=UTF-8" />
```

The JavaScript programming instructions are stored in a separate file called en_jsint.js and called into the web page.

```
<script language="javascript" src = "en_jsint.js">
</script>
</head>
<body bgcolor="lightyellow" onLoad = "cursorload()">
<form name="one" id = "one" method = "post" accept-
charset="iso-8859-1, utf-8">
action = "/cgi-main/gform" onSubmit="return
checkform()">
<br />Please complete the following:
```

```
<table>
<tr>
<td>Family Name:
<input type="text" name="fname" id = "fname"
size="40" /></td>
</tr>
<tr>
<td>Given Name:
<input type="text" name="gname" id = "gname"
size="40" /></td>
</tr>
<tr>
<td>Address: <input type="text" name="address1" id =
"address3" size="30" /></td>
</tr>
<tr>
<td>Address: <input type="text" name="address2" id =
"address3" size="30" /></td>
</tr>
<tr>
<td>Address: <input type="text" name="address3" id =
"address3" size="30" /></td>
</tr>
<tr>
<td>City: <input type="text" name="city" id = "city"
size="30" /></td>
</tr>
<tr>
<td>State, Province, Prefecture: <input type="text"
name="region" id = "region" size="50" /></td>
</tr>
<tr>
<td>Postal Code: <input type="text" name="postal" id
= "postal" size="30" /></td>
</tr>
<tr>
<td><select name="countries" id = "countries"
onChange="selecting('document.one.countries','documen
t.one.t1')">
  <option value="">Select A Country</option>
  <option value="Greece">Greece</option>
  <option value="Holland">Holland</option>
  <option value="South Korea">South Korea</option>
  <option value="Vietnam">Vietnam</option>
</select><br />
```

```
<tr><td>Country
<input type="text" name="t1" id = "t1" value=""></td>
</tr>
<tr>
<td>Email: <input type="text" name="email" id =
"email"size="30" /></td>
</tr>
<tr>
<td>Phone: <input type="text" name="phone" id =
"phone" size="30" / ></td>
</tr>
<tr>
<td>Fax: <input type="text" name="fax" id = "fax"
size="30" /></td>
</tr>
<tr />
<tr /><tr><td>Enter your billing address
here</td><td>
<textarea name="billto" id = "billto" cols="40"
rows="4" onChange="CopyAddress()">
</textarea>
<input type="checkbox" name="same" id = "same"
onClick="CopyAddress()">
Ship to Billing Address</td></tr><tr><td>Enter your
shipping address here</td><td>
<textarea name="shipto" id = "shipto" cols=40 rows=4
onChange="CopyAddress()">
</textarea></td></tr>
<tr>
<td ><b><font size="4" color="blue">Which Video Do
You Want?</font></b></td>
</tr>
<tr>
<td><input type="radio" name="video" id = "radio"
value="training" />
<b><font color="#0000CC"> Leash Training
</font></b></td>
<td><input type="radio" name="video" id = "video"
value="potty" />
<b><font color="#0000CC"> House Breaking
</font></b></td>
<td><input type="radio" name="video" id = "video"
value="none" />
<b><font color="#0000CC"> None</font></b></td>
```

```
</tr>
<tr />
<tr>
<td ><b><font size="4" color="blue">Which Book Do You
Want?</font></b></td>
</tr>
<tr>
<td ><input type="checkbox" name="carole" id =
"carole" value="carole" />
<font face="Paris, Arial Narrow, Arial"
size="3"><b><font color="#0000CC">My Dog
Carole</font></b></font>
</td>
<td ><input type="checkbox" name="hedy" id = "hedy"
value="hedy" />
<font face="Paris, Arial Narrow, Arial"
size="3"><b><font color="#0000CC">My Dog
Hedy</font></b></font></td>
<td ><input type="checkbox" name="none" id = "none"
value="none" />
<font face="Paris, Arial Narrow, Arial"
size="3"><b><font color="#0000CC">None
</font></b></font></td>
</tr>
</table>
<input type="submit" value="Send Your Order" /><input
type = "clear" value = "Clear the Form" />
</form>
</body>
</html>
```

En_jsint.js (code)

This function is called when the page loads into the user's computer.
It is called by the event handler onLoad in the open body tag. The
instructions contained in the function place the cursor in the family
name field. Focus() is a method that automatically places the cursor
in a specific field.

```
function cursorload()
{
document.one.fname.focus()
}
```

This function is called by the event handler onChange. If the user says that the billing address is the same as the shipping address, then the contents of the two fields are made the same.

```
function CopyAddress()
  {
   if (document.one.same.checked)
  {
    document.one.shipto.value = document.one.billto.
value;
   }
}
```

This function is called when the user tries to send off the filled in form to the server. It runs several checks.

```
function checkform()
{
```

This sets up variables to prevent a lot of typing.

```
var famname=document.one.fname.value;
var femail=document.one.email.value;
var fphone=document.one.phone.value;
var fcity=document.one.city.value;
var fax=document.one.fax.value;
var i=0;
var x=0;
```

*If the family name box is empty, this prompts the user to fill in a name.

```
if (famname=="")
   {alert("Please enter your name");
   document.one.fname.focus();
   return false;
}
```

If the city box is empty, this prompts the user to fill in a city.

```
if(fcity=="")
{alert("Please enter your city")
document.one.city.focus()
return false;
}
```

If the e-mail box is empty, this prompts the user to fill in an e-mail address.

```
if (femail==")
  {
alert("Please enter your email address");
  document.one.email.focus();
  return false;}
```

This checks to see if an @ symbol and a period are entered. It also checks to make sure that there are no spaces in the e-mail address and that it is at least six characters long. The characters entered into a text field are regarded as a string object. IndexOf is a method belonging to the string object that tells you at what position a specific character is in a string. It starts counting the characters at zero. If the string does not contain the character, –1 is the result. The double vertical line between each condition sets each condition apart in the browser's mind as a separate check, but also tells the browser to do each one.

```
if (femail!="")
{if (femail.indexOf("@")==-1 ||
femail.indexOf(".")==-1 ||
femail.indexOf(" ")!=-1 ||
femail.length<6)
{
alert("Sorry, your email address is not valid. Please
enter a correct e-mail address such as lmain@wahoo.
sjsu.edu.us");
document.one.email.focus();
return false
}
}
```

This checks to see that something is entered into the phone field. Then it does a further check to make sure that what is entered into the phone field is limited to the following characters: 0123456789()-+.

```
if (fphone=="")
  {
alert("Please enter your Phone Number");
  document.one.phone.focus();
  return false;
}
        var GoodChars = "0123456789()-+ "
for (i =0; i <= fphone.length -1; i++)
{
```

```
if (GoodChars.indexOf(fphone.charAt(i)) == -1)
{alert(fphone.charAt(i) + " Cannot be used in a phone
number. Please enter a correct phone number.")
return false        .

}
}
```

This checks to make sure that one of the radio buttons is selected.

```
count = -1
for (var i=0;i<document.one.video.length; i++)
{
if (document.one.video[i].checked)
{
count = 1
}
}
  if (count ==-1)
{
alert("You must choose a video or select None");
      return false;
}
```

This checks to make sure that one of the checkboxes is selected.

```
var i= (document.one.carole.checked || document.one.
hedy.checked || document.one.none.checked)
if (!i)
  {
alert("Choose at least one diva dog to win or select
None.")
return false
}
```

This ensures that a selection is made from the drop down list.

```
if (document.one.countries.selectedIndex == 0)
{
alert("You must select a country")
document.one.countries.focus()
return false
}
}
```

This takes the selection from the drop down list and enters it into a text box.

7

XML, XSLT, and SVG

XML was briefly discussed in chapter 5. It is important to remember that it is different from XHTML in that it is used to handle data that can be defined in a structured format and that follow a repeating pattern. Also, you have to do a lot more work in XML than in HTML or XHTML. As there are no preset tags, the designer must create tags, or elements, that will enable users to access the content in a useful way. The creation of tags or elements is called making a document type definition, or DTD. This in itself is evolving into schemas. Creating a DTD can be a complex task requiring a good understanding of a discipline or a topic and its internal relationships.

There is actually no need to create a DTD in order to work with XML. Two types of XML documents are possible: well-formed XML and valid XML. A well-formed XML document merely follows syntax rules, such as making sure that all tags are closed, that all attributes are enclosed in quotation marks, and that capitalization is correct. In one sense, a well-formed XML file is not much different from an XHTML file, as it just contains cleanly marked up text. The advantage over XHTML is that an XML file can work with XSLT and display information in a meaningful way, as discussed in chapter 5.

An XML document validates its elements or tags against a DTD (this includes checking that parent–child relationships are respected) before the stylesheet displays the data. Despite the work involved, it is best to use a DTD and create valid XML files. The reason is that you will create a formal description of the XML data and carefully think through the structure of the information and its relationships. A DTD enables groups of XML documents to share a common vocabulary and thus makes it easier to exchange, process, and display XML data across many organizations.

After the DTD is created and the data is coded using the newly created tags or elements, the next step is to think about how to present and access the coded data. Unlike XHTML, XML has no way to present information. Therefore, the final task is to hide the tags or elements by designing an interface using a stylesheet language like CSS or XSLT. XSLT is very powerful. It provides not only the ability to display coded XML but also database search and sorting capabilities. Thus, one set of data can be sorted and displayed in many different ways.

HOW DOES XSLT WORK?

XSLT transforms XML documents into something that the browser can display, which is currently HTML or XHTML. As part of that transformation, one can filter and sort XML data. Also, as a component of this process, XSLT permits the formatting of XML documents using HTML and CSS.

Working with the browser XSLT examines the XML file and creates a hierarchical tree (called a node tree). A node is each individual element or tag of the XML file. Then the browser looks for instructions about what to do with each piece of the tree. The instructions are contained in templates in the XSLT file. Each template has two parts: a label that identifies the nodes to which the template is to be applied and the actual instructions at to how the information should look.

Figures 7.1 to 7.4 illustrate the parts that make up the XML experience. Figure 7.1 shows a sample DTD. Figure 7.2 shows an XML file marked up with the DTD elements. Figure 7.3 shows an interface for the XML file using XSLT. Figure 7.4 shows a different XSLT interface using the same XML file.

```
<!ELEMENT cdlist (cd*)>
<!ELEMENT cd (title, performer+, composer+, publisher)>
<!ELEMENT title (#PCDATA)>
<!ELEMENT performer (main+, assisting*)>
<!ELEMENT main (#PCDATA)>
<!ELEMENT assisting (#PCDATA)>
<!ELEMENT composer (name, composition+)>
<!ELEMENT name (#PCDATA)>
<!ELEMENT composition (unittitle*, movement*)>
<!ELEMENT unittitle (#PCDATA)>
<!ELEMENT movement (#PCDATA)>
<!ELEMENT publisher (corpname, label,year)>
<!ELEMENT corpname (#PCDATA)>
<!ELEMENT label (#PCDATA)>
<!ELEMENT year (#PCDATA)>
```

Figure 7.1

```
<?xml version="1.0" ?>
<!DOCTYPE cdlist (View Source for full doctype...)>
<cdlist>
<cd>
  <title>Karita Mattila</title>
<performer>
  <main>Mattila, Karita - soprano</main>
  <assisting>Lahti Symphony Orchestra</assisting>
  <assisting>Soderblom, Ulf - conductor</assisting>
  </performer>
<composer>
  <name>Paul Hindemith</name>
  <composition>
  <unittitle>Das Marienleben</unittitle>
  <movement>Geburt Maria</movement>
  <movement>Vom Tode Maria</movement>
  </composition>
  </composer>
<publisher>
  <corpname>Fazer Music Inc.</corpname>
  <label>Finlandia Records</label>
  <year>1988</year>
  </publisher>
  </cd>
</cdlist>
```

Figure 7.2

Finn-Classicals on CD

TITLE	PERFORMER	RECORD LABEL
Karita Mattila	Mattila, Karita - soprano	Fazer Music Inc.
The Celebrated Soprano SOILE ISOKOSKI	Isokoski, Soile - soprano	Fazer Music Inc.
Jorma Hynninen	Hynninen, Jorma - Baritone	Fazer Music Inc.
Kaija Saariaho: Private Gardens	Hoitenga, Camilla - flute	Ondine Inc.
Sallinen: String Quartets 1-5	Jean Sibelius Quartet	Ondine Inc.
Saariaho: Maa	Tapio Tuomola - conductor	Ondine Inc.

Figure 7.3   Note that this stylesheet is programmed to show only the title, the performer, and the record label.

Finn-Classicals : Composer Listing

CD TITLE: **Karita Mattila**

> Composer: **Paul Hindemith**
>
> Composer: **Aulis Sallinen**
>
> Composer: **Aarre Merikanto**

CD TITLE: **The Celebrated Soprano SOILE ISOKOSKI**

> Composer: **Paul Hindemith**
>
> Composer: **Ture Rangstrom**
>
> Composer: **Toivo Kuula**
>
> Composer: **Edvard Grieg**

CD TITLE: **Jorma Hynninen**

Figure 7.4   Note that this stylesheet is programmed to show only the title and the composers.

HOW CAN XML AND XSLT HELP WITH DESIGNING AND BUILDING WEBSITES FOR AN INTERNATIONAL AUDIENCE?

If the layout of a collection of documents is very similar (apart from the fact that the documents are in a variety of languages), XML offers the possibility of building and maintaining a single XML file. A variety of different stylesheets can present the parts of the data that are in a specific language. Therefore, XML lets the website designer build one data set and several different interfaces for that data set. The three parts—a sample DTD file, a sample XML file, and a sample XSLT file—are discussed in the following sections.

Language.dtd

```
<!ELEMENT languages (language*)>
<!ELEMENT language (title, firstname,
lastname,prefix,suffix, address1, address2,
address3, city, region, areacode, telephone,
submit, lang, charset,langname)>
<!ATTLIST language xml:lang CDATA #REQUIRED>
<!ATTLIST language engname CDATA #REQUIRED>
<!ATTLIST language langname CDATA #REQUIRED>
<!ATTLIST language charset CDATA #REQUIRED>
<!ELEMENT title (#PCDATA)>
<!ELEMENT firstname (#PCDATA)>
<!ELEMENT lastname (#PCDATA)>
<!ELEMENT prefix (#PCDATA)>
<!ELEMENT suffix (#PCDATA)>
<!ELEMENT address1 (#PCDATA)>
<!ELEMENT address2 (#PCDATA)>
<!ELEMENT address3 (#PCDATA)>
<!ELEMENT city (#PCDATA)>
<!ELEMENT region (#PCDATA)>
<!ELEMENT postalcode (#PCDATA)>
<!ELEMENT areacode (#PCDATA)>
<!ELEMENT telephone (#PCDATA)>
<!ELEMENT submit (#PCDATA)>
<!ELEMENT lang (#PCDATA)>
<!ELEMENT charset (#PCDATA)>
<!ELEMENT langname (#PCDATA)>
```

1. Start by defining the root element (languages) and the elements contained within it (language). The asterisk (*) means that the language element can be repeated as many times as you want. When you look at the data (see the following section, entitled "Language.xml"), note that the whole file is wrapped within languages (open and closed). Each individual entry is wrapped with language (open and closed).

2. If the content between tags or elements (called element content) is data, as opposed to other elements, it is defined as parsed character data (PCDTA).
3. Elements can contain attributes. Attributes are like adjectives in that they enhance what you can describe with an element. This is a means of adding supplementary data to the element. There has been some debate as to whether to use attributes, which could just be separate elements. Either way is fine. Elements are better for information that you want to display; attributes are better for information about information. For each attribute, you define the type (meaning the kind of data). CDATA defines the attribute as containing any kind of characters except elements. #REQUIRED means that the attribute value must be filled in.
4. The DTD is saved as a separate file called language.dtd and called from within the XML file. Note below how it is called into the XML file using <!DOCTYPE languages SYSTEM "language.dtd">. The name of the DTD must be the same as the root element. The name is the part that follows the word *DOCTYPE.*

Language.xml

Note the following:

1. The encoding is set to UTF-8. Individual encoding can also be set for different languages if so desired.
2. The DTD is called into the file.
3. The stylesheet is called into the file.
4. The root element <languages> wraps the whole file.
5. The element <language> wraps each individual entry.
6. Within the element <language>, attributes are set up for each entry to specify the language per the ISO639 codes, the English name of the language, the name of the language (in the language), and a charset.

```
<?xml version="1.0" encoding="UTF-8"?>
<!DOCTYPE languages SYSTEM "language.dtd">
<?xml-stylesheet type="text/xsl"
href="booklanguage.xsl"?>
```
                              continued on next page

```
<languages>
  <language xml:lang="en" engname="English"
langname="English" charset="Windows-1252">
    <title>Localize ASP with XML</title>
    <firstname>First name</firstname>
    <lastname>Last name</lastname>
    <prefix>Prefix</prefix>
    <suffix>Suffix</suffix>
    <address1>Address</address1>
    <address2>Address 2</address2>
    <address3>Address 3</address3>
    <city>City</city>
    <region>State/Province</region>
    <postalcode>Postal code</postalcode>
    <areacode>Area code</areacode>
    <telephone>Telephone number</telephone>
    <submit>OK</submit>
    <lang>en</lang>
    <charset>Windows-1252</charset>
    <langname>English</langname>
  </language>
  <language xml:lang="fr" engname="French"
langname="français" charset="Windows-1252">
    <title name= "title">Localize ASP1 with XML -
French</title>
    . . . French information . . .
    <lang>fr</lang>
    <charset name = "charset">Windows-1252
</charset>
    <langname>French</langname>
  </language>
<language xml:lang="fr" engname="French"
langname="français" charset="Windows-1252">
    <title name = "title">Localize ASP2 with XML -
French</title>
        . . . French information . . .
    <lang>fr</lang>
    <charset name = "charset">Windows-1252
</charset>
    <langname>French</langname>
  </language>
```
continued on next page

```
<language xml:lang="fr" engname="French"
langname="franÃ§ais" charset="Windows-1252">
    <title >Localize ASPa with XML - French
</title>
        . . . French information . . .
    <lang>fr</lang>
    <charset >Windows-1252</charset>
    <langname>French</langname>
  </language>
<language xml:lang="fr" engname="French"
langname="franÃ§ais" charset="Windows-1252">
    <title name = "title">Localize ASP3 with XML -
French</title>
        . . . French information . . .
    <lang>fr</lang>
    <charset name = "charset">Windows-1252
</charset>
    <langname>French</langname>
  </language>
  <language xml:lang="es" engname="Spanish"
langname="Espanol" charset="Windows-1252">
      <title>Localize ASP with XML -
Spanish</title>
        . . . Spanish information . . .
    <lang>sp</lang>
    <charset>iso-8859-1</charset>
    <langname>Spanish</langname>
  </language>
  <language xml:lang="el" engname="Greek"
langname="Greek" charset="windows-1253">
    <title>Localize ASP with XML - Greek
</title>
        . . . Greek information . . .
    <lang>el</lang>
    <charset>windows-1253</charset>
    <langname>Greek</langname>
  </language>
  <language xml:lang="ja" engname="Japanese"
langname="Japanese" charset="x-sjis">
```

continued on next page

```
    <title>Localize ASP with XML -
Japanese</title>
    . . . Japanese information . . .
    <lang>ja</lang>
    <charset>x-sjis</charset>
    <langname>Japanese</langname>
  </language>
</languages>
```

Booklanguage.xsl

Booklanguage.xsl is an example of an XSLT stylesheet called into the language.xml file (see figure 7.5).

 Book Sales Report

Localize ASP1 with XML - French
Prénom
Nom
Préfixe (M., Mme, Mlle)
Suffixe/Titre
Rue

Ville
Région/Province
Code postal
Indicatif régional
Numéro de téléphone
OK
fr
Windows-1252
French

Figure 7.5

Since an XSL stylesheet is an XML file itself, the file begins with an XML declaration. The xsl:stylesheet element indicates that this document is a stylesheet. Then you define the version of the stylesheet, open the stylesheet, and define the namespace. A namespace lets you mix elements drawn from different DTDs within the same XML file. See the discussion on namespaces in the appendix to chapter 5.

```
<xsl:stylesheet version="1.0" xmlns:xs/="http.//www.
w3.org/1999/xsl/Transform">
```

Here the code refers to the root element or tag (or node) of the XML source document. It then goes on to define how the framework of the document should look. It will typically be displayed as an XHTML document. The root template can contain literal elements that are output as is (they are usually XHTML tags or text or CSS instructions) and instructions as to how to handle the rest of the XML elements (or tags), namely the elements or tags under the root. Note: XSL recognizes certain XHTML tags: <html>, <title>, <meta>, <script> (and thus all JavaScript), <style> (and thus all CSS), <body>, <div>, <span>, <br>, <img>, <a>, <form>, <input>, <select>, <textarea>, <hr>, <table>, <caption>, <col>, <colgroup>, <tbody>, <tfoot>, <tr>, and <td>. This template closes further down.

```
<xsl:template match="/">
<html>
<head>
<title>Book Sales Report</title>
<style type="text/css">
body {font-family:Tahoma,Arial,sans-serif;
font-size:10pt; font-weight:normal;
line-height:140%}
.heading {font-family:Tahoma,Arial,sans-serif;
font-size:16pt; font-weight:bold}
.over {font-family:Tahoma,Arial,sans-serif;
font-size:11pt; font-weight:bold}
.under {font-family:Tahoma,Arial,sans-serif;
font-size:11pt; color:red;
font-weight:bold}
</style>
</head>
<body>
<div class="heading">
<img src="books.gif" align="bottom" hspace="10" />
Book Sales Report
</div>
<hr />
```

The xsl:for-each element tells the browser to process information for each piece of data wrapped within <languages/language/> or, in other words, language and all its children. In this case, we are limiting the selection to those entries that are in French. The @ means attribute and refers to the attribute added to the language element. Make sure you close the <xsl:for-each further down.

```
<xsl:for-each select="languages/language[@xml:
lang='fr']">
```

The children you want displayed are listed next, in this case, all the elements. If you only wanted to display some of the elements, then you would just list those.

```
<xsl:apply-templates />
<hr />
</xsl:for-each>
</body>
</html>
```

End of root template section

```
</xsl:template>
```

This is where you specify exactly how you want the data in the tags listed above to display. In this example, you want each child to look the same so you can use the *. The next stylesheet shows how to vary the presentation of each element.

```
<xsl:template match="*">
```

Xsl:value-of select is where the data gets associated with the elements or tags in the display. The xsl:value-of element selects a child in the hierarchy and inserts the content of that child into the template. In this case, it says insert all the data for each element or tag.

```
<b><xsl:value-of select = ."" /></b><br />
</xsl:template>
</xsl:stylesheet>
```

Booklanguage1.xsl

This stylesheet presents the same data with a different interface (see figure 7.6). Since an XSL stylesheet is an XML file itself, the file begins with an XML declaration. The xsl:stylesheet element indicates that this document is a stylesheet. Then you define the version of the stylesheet, open the stylesheet, and define the namespace.

A List of Books

Localize ASP1 with XML - French:	"*French*"	Last Name: **Nom** First Name: **Prénom**
Localize ASP2 with XML - French:	"*French*"	Last Name: **Nom** First Name: **Prénom**
Localize ASPa with XML - French:	"*French*"	Last Name: **Nom** First Name: **Prénom**
Localize ASP3 with XML - French:	"*French*"	Last Name: **Nom** First Name: **Prénom**

Figure 7.6

```
<?xml version="1.0"?>
<xsl:stylesheet version="1." xmlns: xsl=
"http://www.w3.org/1999/xsl/Transform"
```

Here the code refers to the root element or tag (or node) of the XML source document. It then goes on to define how the framework of the document should look. It will typically be displayed as an XHTML document. The root template can contain literal elements that are output as is (they are usually XHTML tags or text or CSS instructions) and instructions as to how to handle the rest of the XML elements (or tags), namely the elements or tags under the root. Note: XSL recognizes certain XHTML tags. They are <html>, <title>, <meta>, <script> (and thus all JavaScript), <style> (and thus all CSS), <body>, <div>, <span>, <br>, <img>, <a>, <form>, <input>, <select>, <textarea>, <hr>, <table>, <caption>, <col>, <colgroup>, <tbody>, <tfoot>, <tr>, and <td>. This template closes further down.

```
<xsl:template match="/">
<html>
<body>
<div style="font-family:Tahoma,Arial,sans-serif;
font-size:24pt; color:green;
text-align:center; letter-spacing:8px;
font-weight:bold">
A List of Books
</div>
<hr />
<table width="100%" cellpadding="5">
```

The xsl:for-each element tells the browser to process information for each piece of data wrapped within <languages/language /> or, in other words, language and all its children. In this case, we are limiting the selection to those entries that are in French. The @ means attribute and refers to the attribute added to the language element. Make sure you close the <xsl:for-each further down.

```
<xsl:for-each select="languages/language[@xml:
lang='fr']">
```

The children you want displayed are listed next. In this case, you only want to display title, language name, last name, and firstname.

```
<tr>
<xsl:apply-templates select="title" />
<xsl:apply-templates select="langname" />
<xsl:apply-templates select="lastname" />
</tr>
<tr>
<xsl:apply-templates select="firstname" />
</tr>
<tr><td colspan="3"><hr /></td></tr>
</xsl:for-each>
</table>
<div style="font-family:Arial,sans-serif;
font-size:8pt; margin-left:10px">
</div>
</body>
</html>
```

End of root template section

```
</xsl:template>
```

<xsl:template-match /> is where you specify exactly how you want the data in the tags listed above to display. The following example varies the presentation of a couple of the elements. The xsl:value-of select is where the data gets associated with the elements or tags in the display. The xsl:value-of element selects a child in the hierarchy and inserts the content of that child into the template. In this case it says insert all the data for each element or tag.

```
<xsl:template match="title">
<td rowspan="2"
style="font-family:Comic Sans MS, Arial,sans-serif;
color:darkblue; font-size:16pt;
font-weight:bold">
```

```
<xsl:value-of select = ."" />:
</td>
</xsl:template>
<xsl:template match="langname">
<td rowspan="2"
style="font-family:Lucida Handwriting
Italic,Arial,sans-serif;
font-size:18pt; font-weight:bold; color:darkred">
"<xsl:value-of select = ."" />"</td>
</xsl:template>
<xsl:template match="firstname">
<td style="font-family:Tahoma,Arial,sans-serif;
font-size:10pt">
First Name: <b><xsl:value-of select = ."" /></b>
</td>
</xsl:template>
<xsl:template match="lastname">
<td style="font-family:Tahoma,Arial,sans-serif;
font-size:10pt">
Last Name: <b><xsl:value-of select = ."" /></b>
</td>
</xsl:template>
</xsl:stylesheet>
```

Figure 7.7 shows the result if we set the attribute in the stylesheet to Greek: <xsl:for-each select="languages/language [@xml:lang='el']">.

A List of Books

Localize ASP with XML - Greek: *"Greek"*   Last Name: **Επώνυμο**
                                                          First Name: **Όνομα**

Figure 7.7

PROGRAMMING CAPABILITIES OF XSLT

Using the xml:lang attribute and the lang() function of an XSL stylesheet, it is possible to store all XML data in one file and all element name translations in a second XML file and apply one stylesheet to display element names and data based on language. Figure 7.8 presents a partial screen shot of an XML file that uses

```
<?xml version="1.0" encoding="utf-8"?>
<?xml:stylesheet type="text/xsl" href="find.xsl"?>
<books>
        <book xml:lang = "en">
                <authorfirstname size="30">James</authorfirstname>
                <authorlastname size="30">Joyce</authorlastname>
                <price size="10">USD 25</price>
                <title size="40">Dubliners</title>
        </book>
<book xml:lang = "fr">
                <authorfirstname size="30">James</authorfirstname>
                <authorlastname size="30">Joyce</authorlastname>
                <price size="10">15 EURO</price>
                <title size="40">Portraite d'Artiste Un Jeune Homme</title>
        </book>
<book xml:lang = "en">
                <authorfirstname size="30">James</authorfirstname>
                <authorlastname size="30">Joyce</authorlastname>
                <price size="10">USD 25</price>
                <title size="40">Portrait of the Artist As A Young Man</title>
        </book>
</books>
```

Figure 7.8

xml:lang to assign language codes. Notice that it calls the stylesheet find.xsl. If the find.xsl stylesheet is set to English (en), it will work with the XML file shown in figure 7.9 to produce the result shown in figure 7.10. If the stylesheet is set to French (fr), it will produce the result shown in figure 7.11. The find.xsl stylesheet and the XML files can be found at senna.sjsu.edu/lmain/global.

```
<?xml version="1.0" encoding="UTF-8" ?>
- <allheadings>
  - <headings xml:lang="en">
     <heading category="authorfirstname">Author First Name</heading>
     <heading category="authorlastname">Author Last Name</heading>
     <heading category="price">Price</heading>
     <heading category="title">Title</heading>
    </headings>
  - <headings xml:lang="fr">
     <heading category="authorfirstname">Prenom</heading>
     <heading category="authorlastname">Deuxieme Nom</heading>
     <heading category="price">Prix</heading>
     <heading category="title">Titre</heading>
    </headings>
  </allheadings>
```

Figure 7.9

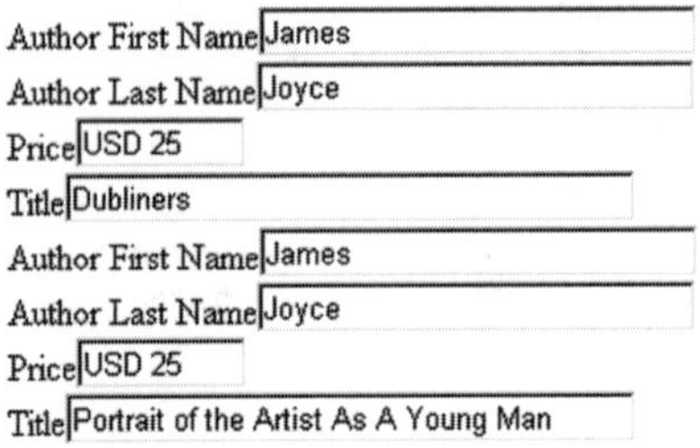

Author First Name	James
Author Last Name	Joyce
Price	USD 25
Title	Dubliners
Author First Name	James
Author Last Name	Joyce
Price	USD 25
Title	Portrait of the Artist As A Young Man

Figure 7.10

Prenom	James
Deuxieme Nom	Joyce
Prix	15 EURO
Titre	Portraite d'Artiste Un Jeune Homme

Figure 7.11

It is possible to use JavaScript to change the language values dynamically by passing the value of the desired language parameter to the stylesheet. It is also possible to modify the program so that each XML content file is kept in a language specific directory (rather than using one large file with items marked with xml:lang).[1]

USING THE DOM

One can use a series of small XHTML files to call the XML file, the DTD, and the relevant language stylesheet, as in the following example. Fundamentally, DOM is the concept of the browser viewing the web page as a collection of objects that can be accessed and manipulated. In this program, empty (unseen) objects are created into which we can load the XML file, the DTD, and the stylesheet. Figure 7.12 presents the result.

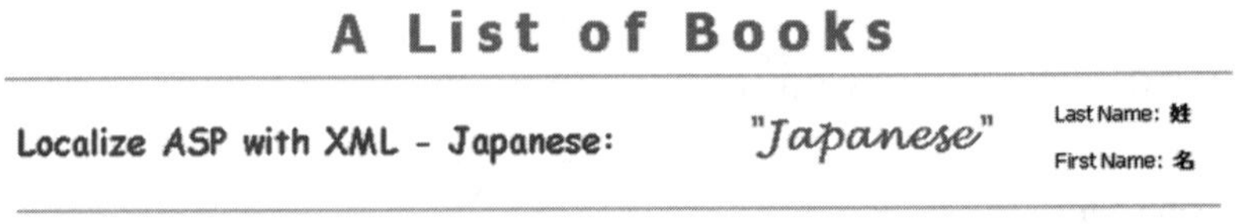

A List of Books

Localize ASP with XML - Japanese: "Japanese"   Last Name: 姓
First Name: 名

Figure 7.12

Dom.html

```
<html>
<body>
<script language="javaScript">
// Load DTD
var dtd = new ActiveXObject("Microsoft.XMLDOM")
dtd.async = false
dtd.load("language.dtd")
// Load XML
var dtd = new ActiveXObject("Microsoft.XMLDOM")
dtd.async = false
dtd.load("language.xml")
// Load the XSL
var xsl = new ActiveXObject("Microsoft.XMLDOM")
xsl.async = false
xsl.load("japanlanguage.xsl")
<!—This is the same stylesheet as above, but with
xml:lang = "ja"→
// Transform
document.write(xml.transformNode(xsl))
</script>
</body>
</html>
```

By further manipulating the DOM, the website designer can offer searching capabilities based on the language of the user. For instance, the user selects a language from the drop down box (see figure 7.13) (discussed in chapters 5 and 6). If, for example, the user selects French,

Figure 7.13

the browser will take him or her to a search page in French, where the user will type in the search phrase (see figure 7.14). The stylesheet will search through the XML file, isolate material where the xml:lang attribute is set to fr, and bring up the French titles that match (see figure 7.15). Figures 7.16 and 7.17 present the interface in Spanish.

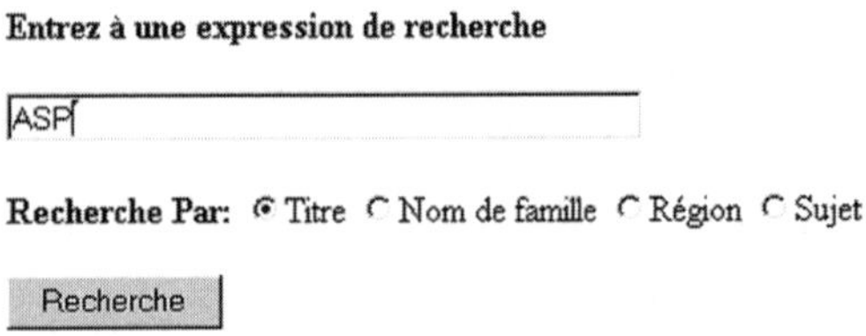

Entrez à une expression de recherche

```
ASP
```

Recherche Par: ⦿ Titre ◌ Nom de famille ◌ Région ◌ Sujet

[Recherche]

Figure 7.14

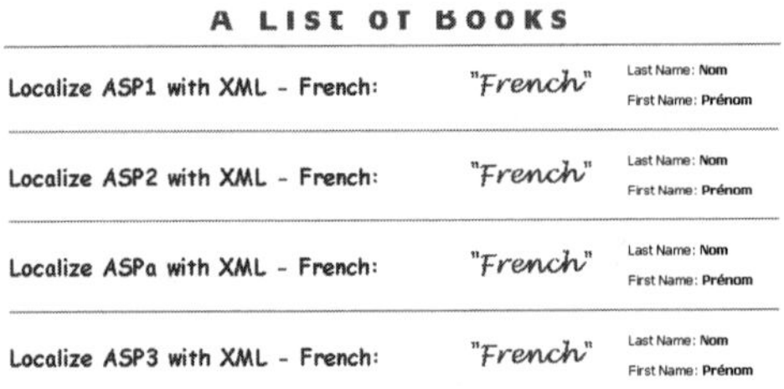

A LIST OF BOOKS

Localize ASP1 with XML - French:	*"French"*	Last Name: **Nom** First Name: **Prénom**
Localize ASP2 with XML - French:	*"French"*	Last Name: **Nom** First Name: **Prénom**
Localize ASPa with XML - French:	*"French"*	Last Name: **Nom** First Name: **Prénom**
Localize ASP3 with XML - French:	*"French"*	Last Name: **Nom** First Name: **Prénom**

Figure 7.15

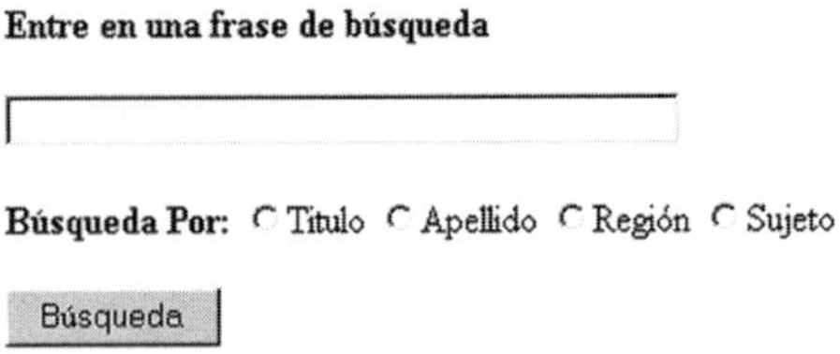

Entre en una frase de búsqueda

```
```

Búsqueda Por: ◌ Titulo ◌ Apellido ◌ Región ◌ Sujeto

[Búsqueda]

Figure 7.16

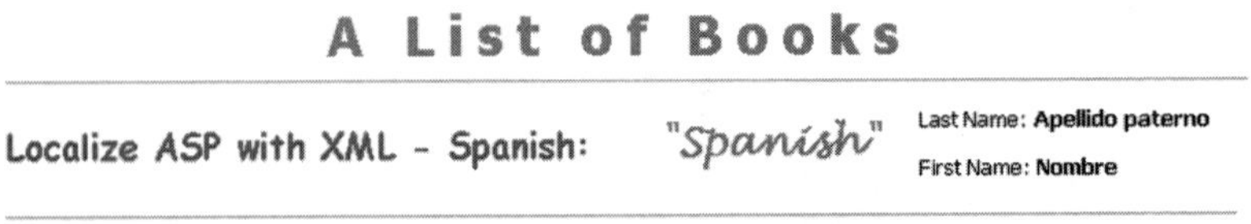

A List of Books

Localize ASP with XML - Spanish:	*"Spanish"*	Last Name: **Apellido paterno** First Name: **Nombre**

Figure 7.17

SCALABLE VECTOR GRAPHICS

Different markup languages (or DTDs) have been developed for specific disciplines. One of the most potentially useful for building multinational web pages is scalable vector graphics (SVG) markup language. SVG is an XML format for marking up graphical data.

Graphics currently used on web pages (typically .gif or .jpeg formats) are pixel-based (or raster) graphics. Pixel-based graphics distort if you try to resize them on the fly. Vector-based graphics are made up of instructions rather than pixels. They are mathematical descriptions of an image rendered on a computer screen by a browser that reads the description and builds the image. Currently, the browser needs the help of a plug-in, such as the Adobe SVG Viewer.[2]

Since SVG[3] is an XML format, several XSLT stylesheets can be applied to the one file to tailor appearances for different situations. For example, a user could click on a button to change the text between English and another language of choice. The stylesheet could make the button smaller or larger without any distortion. JavaScript could be used to ensure that changing the language also changed the destination of the navigation buttons (to the appropriate language directory on the server). A content developer might easily embed an unusual font enabling text to be rendered as intended without making assumptions about the user's available fonts.

Files created in SVG are smaller than pixel-based files, as they are merely text instructions. SVG, as an XML format, supports Unicode and CSS2 features, such as vertical, vertical ideographic (the writing mode feature), and bidirectional text (the direction and unicode-bidi features). Two examples that illustrate the potential of SVG are *Hiragana Quiz*, which can be found at www.kenjikojima. com/HiraganaQuiz and *A Demo with Asian Characters*, which can be found at kyip2asia.com/samples3.htm. Kevin Lindsey illustrates how SVG can be linked to mp3 sound files at www.kevlindev.com/samples/overlord/index.htm. This offers the potential of welcoming a user to the web page in his or her language. The above URLs can also be accessed from senna.sjsu.edu/lmain/global.

NOTES

1. David Silverlight, "Shedding a Little Light on XML" at www.xml-journal.com (accessed March 1, 2002).

2. See www.adobe.com/svg/viewer/install.

3. The following discuss SVG and provide samples and tutorials: Vincent Hardy, "Scalable Vector Graphics (SVG): An Executive Summary" at www.sun.com/software/xml/developers/svg (accessed March 1, 2002); SVG Zone at www.adobe.com/svg/community/external.html (accessed March 1, 2002).

REFERENCES

Cox, Ken. "Multilingual Web Pages with ASP and XML" at www.xmlzone.com/articles/kc1100/cox01-1.asp (accessed March 1, 2002).

"DXML Goes Global: Localization and the XML/DHTML Menus," 1999, at msdn.microsoft.com/library/default.asp?url=/library/enus/dncodecorn/html/corner080999.asp (accessed March 1, 2002).

Ishida, Richard. "XML DTD & Schema Internationalisation" at www.xeroxemea.com/globaldesign/free.htm#dtds (accessed March 1, 2002).

Savourel, Yves. "XML Technologies and the Localization Process." *Multilingual Computing and Technology* 11, 7 (October/November 2000) at www.multilingual.com (accessed March 1, 2002).

Savourel, Yves. *XML: Internationalization and Localization.* Indianapolis, Ind.: Sams, 2001.

8

The Final Test

Thomas Powell describes website usability as allowing the user to manipulate a website's features to accomplish a particular goal.[1] Much has been written about usability and usability testing for web pages.[2] Emphasis is placed on ease of use, understandability, and the importance of gathering information about user characteristics, such as age, gender, and educational level. However, very few usability studies or usability guidelines specifically discuss global usability.[3] The work of Dr. Shirley Becker and Florence E. Mottay at Florida Institute of Technology is significant in that her E3 group has developed a web usability assessment model incorporating over 100 usability elements, which include internationalization and localization issues like native language, semantics (sentence structure and writing style), syntax, local terminology, customs, images, and symbols.[4]

The usability model developed by Dr. Becker and her group stresses the importance of design consistency across all web pages. Each page—whether only internationalized or internationalized and localized—should have a common look and feel. Particular pages can be localized to meet a locality's cultural needs, but they should still retain the common look and feel. The usability assessment model actively examines the impact of cultural differences in design layout, textual organization, and information content. It stresses that page layout usability must pay attention to the significance of colors, the use of graphics, and the placement of text. Navigation must include access to other country sites from the home page, and all access points should be written in native languages. In localized pages, labels, prompts, error messages, and help should be in the local language. If the site includes a search engine, it should be able to search on non-English words.

Multicultural users must be involved in usability testing in order to ensure the success of the web pages. Success means universal access regardless of one's cultural background.

NOTES

1. Thomas Powell, *Web Design: The Complete Reference* (Berkeley, Calif.: Osborne McGraw Hill: 2000).

2. Alison Head, "Design Wise," *Information Today* (1999); Patrick Lynch and Sarah Horton, "Web Style Guide: Basic Design Principles for Creating Web Sites" at info.med.yale.edu/caim/manual (accessed March 1, 2002); National Cancer Institute, "Web Design and Usability Guidelines" at www.usability.gov/guidelines (accessed March 1, 2002); Jakob Nielsen at www.useit.com (accessed March 1, 2002).

3. Constantine Stephanidis, ed., *User Interfaces for All: Concepts, Methods, and Tools* (Mahwah, N.J.: Lawrence Erlbaum Associates, 2001). See especially the following chapters: Aaron Marcus, "Individual Differences and Inclusive Design" and M. Maybury, "International and Intercultural User Interfaces."

4. Shirley Becker and Florence E. Mottay, "A Global Perspective on Web Site Usability," *IEEE Software* 18, (January–February 2001): 54–61; "E-Usability, Education, and Research" at e3.se.fit.edu (accessed March 1, 2002).

Appendix A
Library Automation Vendors and Unicode Compliance

System	URL	Unicode Compliant
Adlib Library/Adlib Information Systems	www.uk.adlibsoft.com	No
Auto-Graphics	www.auto-graphics.com	No
Bailey Solutions	www.baileysolutions. co.uk	No
Best Seller/ BiblioMondo	www.bibliomondo.com	Yes
Book Systems	www.booksys.com	No
Brodart	www.brodart.com	No
CARL	www.carl.org/tlccarl/ index.asp	CARLweb 3.0: yes. The Kid's Catalog also supports Unicode characters. TLC/CARL introduced a Japanese version of the CARLweb product in July 2001. CARLweb is also available in Spanish, Chinese, Polish, and Russian through Unicode scripting. Field labels are also Unicode-enabled so that search results can be e-mailed easily.
CASPR	www.caspr.com	No
COMPanion	www.goalexandria.com	No
Contec Group International	www.contecds.com	The company does not use Unicode as a standard, but Asian languages can be stored using GB, Big 5, Shift-JIS, etc.

System	URL	Unicode Compliant
		This is selectable at time of entry and when searching.
		The system does have font capabilities for Asian languages, including Thai, Korean, Chinese and Japanese.
		The C2 product line is dynamically multilingual. For instance, you can select the language you wish to operate in, and all screen texts will immediately display in that language. Context-sensitive help is also dynamically multilingual. In the case of the bibliographic record, the material may be cataloged in the language of origin if required. Diacritics are stored using the ALA diacritic codes.
DRA	www.dra.com	DRA's AOS library automation product is covered by Unicode. DRA Find, a Z39.50 GUI for searching several databases simultaneously is also Unicode compliant, as are the company's DRA Classic servers.
Diakon Systems	www.diakonsystems. com	No
Eloquent	www.eloquent-systems. com/index.htm	Eloquent Systems uses a product from jBASE to read and write to disk. jBASE version 4 supports Unicode.
Endeavor	www.endinfosys.com	Endeavor announced in late 2000 that its Voyager integrated library management system has the capacity to convert bibliographic MARC records to the Unicode character set.
		The system is based on "glyph server" technology that converts MARC-format bibliographic records to Unicode characters and then displays those characters on any Internet browser.

System	URL	Unicode Compliant
EOS International	www.eosintl.com	Yes
Epixtech (formerly Ameritech Library Services)	www.epixtech.com	Epixtech started beta testing of its 7.0 version of Horizon Sunrise in June 2001. Unicode enhancements are included in this update. Capabilities include ALA diacritics for both display and editing. The ConnectLib collection also claims to have Unicode capabilities.
Ex Libris	www.exlibris-usa.com	Ex Libris products: yes. The ALEPH 500 software is shipped in 20 different languages to over 600 ALEPH customers in 44 different countries. Customers include the Russian National Library, Beijing University, and the Hebrew University in Jerusalem.
Follet Software	www.fsc.follett.com	No
Fretwell-Dowing Informatics	www.fdgroup.co.uk/fdi/ company/home.html	No
Gaylord	www.gaylord.com/ automation	No
Geac	www.library.geac.com	The VubisSm@rt product: yes. It is available in English, French, and Dutch. Geac does not currently have font capability for Asian languages.
Inmagic	www.inmagic.com	No
Innovative Interfaces	www.iii.com	The Millennium products: yes. They can display data in multiple character sets in a single screen. The company also offers an optional Foreign Language Interface module to set a default language, such as French, Chinese, Japanese, Portuguese, Spanish, Thai, and Welsh for OPAC and staff menus. These can be changed with a single keystroke.

System	URL	Unicode Compliant
		Millennium also supports the input, display, and indexing of data in various languages and scripts. The company developed special indexing to support the proper sorting of diacritics for special languages, such as Arabic, Cyrillic, Chinese, Estonian, Hebrew, Polish, Spanish, Swedish, Thai, and Turkish.
Jaywil Software	www.resourcemate.com	No
Kelowna Software	www.L4U.com	No. The OPAC is available in English, French, and Spanish.
Keystone Systems	www.klas.com	No
Open Text, BASIS	www.opentext.com	No
Sagebrush	www.sagebrushcorp. com	No
SIRS Mandarin	www.sirs.com	No. SIRS can be displayed in English, Italian, French, German and Spanish. Circulation is available in English, French and Spanish.
SIRSI	www.sirsi.com	No. SIRSI offers its products in Arabic, Chinese, Spanish, and French. Users can select the language in which they want to search library holdings. The entire screen, including toolbars and buttons, is immediately displayed in the language of choice. Libraries also have the option of providing one particular language at a given workstation. Asian font capabilities are limited to Chinese.
Surpass	www.SurpassSoftware. com	No
Sydney PLUS	www.sydneyplus.com	No
TLC-The Library Corporation	www.tlcdelivers.com	ITS.International has Unicode capability with a transliteration

System	URL	Unicode Compliant
		table that processes the inputted text of any language and generates the equivalent romanized text. Chinese, Japanese, and Korean languages are among those that can be transliterated. The system must be on Windows 2000 for Unicode functionality.
VTLS	www.vtls.com	VTLS is the only library automation company to offer full Unicode support on both the client and server sides.The Unicode capability applies throughout every Virtua subsystem. With a click of a button, a user can access materials using virtually any language, and both left-to-right and right-to-left languages are supported. Full Unicode support only applies to the Windows 2000 operating system (although Virtua is also available under Windows NT). With the NT system, all languages except right-to-left are supported. Virtua is still available for Windows 95 and 98, but VTLS is moving away from Unicode implementation for those versions. VTLS is used by libraries around the world, including the Bibliotheque Cantonale et Universitaire in Fribourg, Switzerland (the library has 85,000 multilingual authority records), Tamkang University in Taiwan (the library has converted its holdings from the Big-5 character set to Unicode. It has holdings in Chinese, Japanese, and Russian as well as the Latin-1 languages), and the University of Campinas in Brazil.

Appendix B
General Resources

Idiom Technologies. "The Globalization Process" at www.idiominc.com/worldwise/implement/con_analyze.asp (accessed March 1, 2002).

Ishida, Richard. "Challenges in Designing International User Information," 1998, at www.xerox-emea.com/globaldesign/paper/paper1.htm (accessed March 1, 2002).

Multilingual Computing and Technology at www.multilingual.com (accessed March 1, 2002).

Web of Culture at www.webofculture.com/worldsmart/toc.asp (accessed March 1, 2002). See especially *WorldSmart.*

Woods, Jordan. "Multilingual Web Site Management" at www.simultrans.com/seminars/seminar200005.htm.

Yunker, John. "Speaking in Charsets. Building a Multilingual Web Site." *WebTechniques,* September 2000, at www.webtechniques.com/archives/2000/09/yunker (accessed March 1, 2002).

Index

About the Author

Linda Main is a professor at San José State University in San José, California, with teaching responsibilities in designing and building websites; web programming languages such as Javascript, XML, and XSL; global internetworking; and history of books and libraries. In this capacity, she has designed and taught several totally online web classes. She has written articles for *Third World Quarterly, Journal of Education for Library and Information Science,* and *Library Software Review.*